SONNETS FROM THE ODYSSEY

D J Etchell holds several qualifications in science
and in classics from various universities. He lives
in splendid seclusion with his wife Jean and dog
Smudge in the North of England.

Also by D J Etchell:

Sonnets from the Iliad
The Lych-Gate: Songs and Sonnets of Autumn

SONNETS FROM THE ODYSSEY

D J Etchell

Burghwallis Books

For my Tutors

Contents

Preface

This book is the never intended sequel to my previous volume, *Sonnets from the Iliad*. Never intended, because after the intense effort of producing the three hundred and seventeen sonnets in that work, I swore that I would never embark on such a task again.

However, on my birthday in March 2009, I made the mistake of picking up the Odyssey and re-reading the opening. Immediately the form of a sonnet sprang into my mind. Thus I embarked on the task and finished it, with an unfinished twelve line sonnet, on sixteenth of October 2009. My computer tells me that there are a total of forty-six thousand, one hundred and sixteen words in this volume. The number is of course increasing slightly as I type. I think I have managed to run through pretty much the whole of the narrative in the Odyssey with very few gaps or omissions. The sequence is far from the whole of the poem, as this runs to twelve thousand, one hundred and ten lines.

I realise that my achievement is less than those poets such as Cowper and Chapman, who did their own translations in addition to reforming Homer's words into English verse. However, I am satisfied with my small contribution to the large number of works which have paid their tributes to the huge genius of this magical poet.

In writing the sequence I used the Richmond Lattimore translation and consulted others from time to time, the principal two being the Loeb as translated by A.T. Murray and revised by George E. Dimock, and that of Ennis Rees. On one occasion I found myself looking through an interesting prose translation done by a certain T.E. Shaw. Once again, Jenny

March's *Dictionary of Classical Mythology* was invaluable in respect of filling in the gaps in my background knowledge.

The writing of the sonnets did cause some annoyance to my dear wife, Jean. This, because most of them were written in bed in the early hours of the morning and not infrequently resulted in ink finding its way onto the duvet cover or pillow slips.

D.J.E.

Book 1

1

Muse! Tell me of the man of those devices
Whose many ruses sought to guide him home;
Who sacked great Troy, then making sacrifices,
Departed, yet for ten years had to roam;
Of his struggles and his god-doomed sailors,
Who blind with folly, perished: fools they were;
Devouring sacred oxen, faithless railers
Against the Sun god's laws—death's feast they share.
Begin, great Zeus' daughter now and tell us,
For all the other heroes had returned;
Alone among them was the cursed Odysseus
Who wandered, while for Ithaca he yearned.
    Calliope, sweet muse! Begin your story
    Of wanderings, adventure and his glory.

2

Snared for seven years by dear Calypso,
Bound by desire within her hollow cave,
Until the circling years decreed he must go
Homewards, free, no longer her love slave.
Pitied by the gods, except Poseidon,
Who to the far off Aithiopes had gone,
His fate decided in those realms Olympian;
Athene said that she would seek his son
And guide him first to Sparta then to Pylos,
To seek for tidings of the king's return,
In hope that he may come, to halt that grave loss
Caused by those feasting there, with no concern.
    With golden sandals then she crossed the sea
    To Ithaka, to stir up destiny.

3

Then disguised as Mentes there she waited
As was the custom, in the outer court;
There sat the suitors with their greed brief sated,
On well scraped Ox hides, playing draughts for sport.
While heralds bustled, laying out the tables
So they could eat with gluttony once more.
Telemachus then saw her near the stables
Standing, waiting, at the outer door.
So drawing near he clasped her hand in welcome,
Ashamed a stranger there, should wait so long;
Thus then with wingéd words he bade her come
Into his hall amid the suitors' throng.
    He sat her there, in honour, mid the feasting
    And saw her served the best of everything.

4

The overbearing suitors sat and dined then
And Phemius, sang for them all—compelled,
While lyre-sweet music occupied those vile men,
Within the son, concern for father welled.
Thus speaking close to flashing eyed Athene,
The noble youth then asked her how she came,
His tide of queries rose about her keenly:
She answered him with guile and gave false name.
She said her ship now lay in Reithron's harbour,
Near Neion, far from the city's eyes,
With iron she'd gone to Temese to barter
For copper in a Taphian lord's disguise.
    She said that old Laertes would attest
    To that bond which was their sire's bequest.

5

Blown by the winds of rumour I am brought here,
For men had said your father had returned.
I prophesy he lives and thus have no fear,
That gods delay him now, will be confirmed;
For he has many wiles and is resourceful,
Thus soon he will contrive a way to come,
He always feels to home his heart strings pull,
Despite what fate and baneful gods have done.
Athene to Odysseus compared him,
Remarking on his head and splendid eyes:
Like those of him who'd left, Troy's walls to win
With all the bravest of the bold Argives.
　　　Since that time she claimed not to have seen
　　　Nor heard of him, or known where he had been.

6

Telemachus said: "no man knows his sire,
But from my mother's clan I'm held as heir,"
Yet broodingly expressed his hearts desire
For lineage which freed him from despair.
"It seems I was begotten of—they say
A sire most cursed by fate of mortal men,"
The goddess though deflected his dismay
And asked of those who drank and feasted then
And acted with such outrage in his halls;
Thus fires of anger she flamed in his heart.
He wished then for that glory which befalls
The hero, fallen, practicing war's art.
　　　Achaians then for him would raise a tomb
　　　And honour to his sons would follow soon.

7

"The harpies though have swept him far away,
And leave me anguished through the suitors greed.
For princes from surrounding isles hold sway
Here in my halls, and wanton, drink and feed.
From Dulchium and Same they have come
And from Zachinthus, here to Ithaca;
They woo my mother in my very home,
While my father wanders near or far.
This stirred anger up in great Athene
Who said: "For him indeed you have much need.
If he were here the suitors would feel keenly
His anger, as his might fell on that breed.
　　Would that the gods now grant his swift return,
　　That he might pay these wastrels what they earn."

8

She said she saw him last in Ephyre,
Where he sought poison for his arrow heads;
Yet Ilus had withheld it through his fear
Of retribution from the mighty gods.
Her father though, through fondness gave it him;
Would that in his full strength he now would come
To pour out vengeance on these princes' sin
For insult to his wife and noble son.
Athene told the youth to now give thought
On how to drive the suitors from his hall,
And call Achea's heroes who had fought
In wars of old to answer to his call.
　　And then to tell those wastrels to depart,
　　While thoughts of marriage filled his mother's heart.

9

Telemachus, she ordered: "Choose a ship!
And with it twenty oarsmen of the best.
Then bound for Pylos let your cables slip
And cross the sea to Nestor without rest.
From there to Sparta and to Menelaus
The last of all Achaeans to reach home;
There you must learn, if indeed Odysseus
Is dead or lives and where he now might roam.
If perished, here return and give those rights
Most fitting in a father's funeral,
And after that prepare to slay those knights
And princes who offend the sight of all.
    For now you stand at manhood's great threshold
    Put youth behind, your time has come, be bold!"

10

The noble prince, there offered her a gift
And then the goddess said she must depart
To search for comrades and their ship so swift,
With plot well woven by her guileful art.
Then skywards flew Athene like a bird
Yet left great courage in his noble heart;
He marvelled at those things which had occurred
Suspecting some great god had played a part.
His hall he entered as a godlike man
As Phemius the famous minstrel sang,
From Troy to home his woeful ballads ran.
Penelope once more felt grief's cruel pang,
    And from her chamber with two maidens fair
    In shining veil descended the high stair.

11

With tearful eyes she heard past sorrow's song
Which brought down grief when sung with lyre, divine.
She bade the minstrel—"choose another one!
Of men and gods, while suitors drink their wine,
For memories come with your soulful words
Of that one, famed from Hellas to Argos."
Telemachus rebuked her mid those lords
That she forbade that song for all their loss.
He ordered her to her loom and distaff: go!
She went then to her chamber high and wept
Whilst uproar broke among that host below;
Each suitor wished that now with her he slept.
    For arrogance her son upbraided them
    And told them all to feast and listen then.

12

"For in the morning our great council meets
And there I will demand that you depart,
To travel home and share in other feasts
For here your greed must ruin's threat impart."
Antinous, the haughty, answered him.
For all were shamed that he should be so bold
And wished the youth should never here be king,
As was his birthright; willed by gods of old.
Telemachus then showed his father's skills
And made good answer then, deflecting him;
Eurymachus declared—soon great Zeus wills
Which lord, in sea-girt Ithaca, is king.
    Yet 'graciously' allowed, that in his home
    The prince could keep those things which were his own.

13

Though curious about where she had gone
They all believed she was indeed Mentes
And turned to drink, and merriment and song,
Then each left for his home to take his ease.
Telemachus though brooded on his fate
As to his bed he went, by tiredness bourn,
In search of rest until the fateful morn.
The wise old servant took his tunic soft
And hung it, smoothed, above the corded bed,
Then closed the door and left him there aloft
To ponder what Athene had just said.
    All through the night wrapped in a warm fleece-skin
    He thought about that journey asked of him.

Book 2

14

Telemachus arose at early dawn,
When rose pale fingers stretched across the sky.
He strode out as a god that early morn
And bade the heralds now to clearly cry,
To summon all Achaeans to the meet;
He went there with bronze spear and two swift hounds
As escorts, either side, behind his feet.
That grace Athene gave him, all astounds,
They marvelled as he came and took his place,
Sat in his father's seat as was his right;
To old Aegyptius then the throng gave space
That he might ask who called them to that site.
    He spoke in hope of news of that great loss:
    Of those who'd sailed with lord Odysseus.

15

The young prince stood to speak and Peisenor,
The herald, placed the staff within his hands;
He spoke of both those evils which he bore
A father's loss as suitors raped his lands.
He spoke then of that shame which all should feel
And warned them of the gods impending ire,
Which Zeus in his great anger would reveal;
He told them all: to mourn, was his desire!
With words of wrath he told them all to leave,
Then dashed the staff down, bursting into tears,
All in silent pity heard him grieve
Until Antinous spoke of those years
    In which his mother, clever in deceit,
    Had used her loom, the suitor's hearts to cheat.

16

She would not wed till finishing that robe
For old Laertes, made there as his shroud,
Then by the daylight at her loom she wove
And yet by night, deceived the suitors proud.
Unpicking what she'd woven there by day
Through the rolling seasons, for three years.
Yet in the fourth we'd learned, to her dismay,
Of her deceit thus now her marriage nears.
A serving woman told us this—compelled,
She's finished that great robe against her will;
Thus let those doubts within you be dispelled
For soon the marriage rite she must fulfil.
    Thus send her to her father who must choose
    A husband here with little time to lose.

17

Penelope has schemed with shrewd device
To keep us off and hold on to your lands,
Thus we will stay and that will be the price
Until she takes one of the suitors hands.
Wisely then Telemachus replied
That he could no way bid his mother go,
Back to her father there to be a bride
With dowry, to all this he must say no!
For evils from the furies would rain down
And others from her father Icarus.
Thus leave my halls and go back to your own
And cease this waste he told Antinous.
    If not I must the gods immortal try
    For now your evils must requital buy.

18

Zeus, far seeing, sent in answer then
Two eagles swooping from a mountain high,
Side by side they flew down to those men
And death was in their glance and fearful cry.
They tore with talons at each others cheeks
Then whirled and left while all in wonder stared;
Halisthernes told all: "That great Zeus wreaks
Revenge—none of the suitors will be spared.
Odysseus now is not so far away,
He comes to sow dark slaughter and red death,
Long years ago I prophesised this day.
He must return fulfilling that old myth,
   He will come in this twentieth year—unknown,
   Without his comrades, back to claim his throne."

19

Eurymachus made mock of what he said,
And told him: "Get back home and prophesy!"
Then stated: "Sure, Odysseus is dead
And your old bones, far off, should near his lie."
Then your vile tongue would not have stirred that anger
Which caused the prince to speak such pride filled words,
For these will bring him grief and lead to danger,
With talk of due return and omened birds.
A fine was threatened if his talk continued
And council there was urged, that with all haste
Penelope should choose from those who there wooed,
Only this would end their drunken waste.
   He said till then the suitors would remain
   And looked on what he'd foretold with disdain.

20

From the prince a wise entreaty came
For twenty comrades and the swiftest ship;
He felt that there he could not now remain
But sought new rumours from some strangers lip.
To find if lord Odysseus was alive,
Or if he'd perished in some far off land.
If there was hope a full year more he'd strive
If none, then he must give his mothers hand.
Mentor rose, rebuking all the rest
For none of them had made the suitors case;
Leocritus said: "foolish your behest,
Who here would take up arms to halt a feast?
 Odysseus himself would surely die
 By force of numbers should he dare to try."

21

Then they scattered, each to his own house,
Except the suitors who returned as one
To Odysseus' halls, there to carouse.
Telemachus though went alone with none
Down to the sea-shore, desolate, to pray.
Athene came again with wingéd words
And told him now to act with no delay
Thus for a while he went to join those lords.
To gather wine in jars, and barley meal,
While she obtained a ship and willing crew.
Again, back to his house he turned his heel,
In troubled mind though, thinking what to do.
 Antinous with mocking welcome came
 Inviting him to feast and there remain.

22

Telemachus then told him he could not
Remain among that haughty, wastrel, crew;
He sought that, vengeance, which the fates allot,
For evil death, was sure the suitors due.
He took his hand back from the mocking man
Yet all the others spoke with jeering talk,
They thought that murder was the young lord's plan,
With men from Pylos brought to do his work
Or from Sparta, perhaps from Ephyre
He would return with poisons for their wine,
As dark thoughts lead those lordlings to conspire.
Those of the prince to his trip's needs incline,
    At his father's store, where Eurycleia,
    The faithful nurse, well guarded all his gear.

23

The young lord asked for covered wine jars: twelve
And barley meal in twenty well sown skins;
Alarmed; the old one asked why he must delve
Where death and danger wait: those deadly twins!
He bound her there to silence, thus she swore
A mighty oath then turned to serve his needs;
Meanwhile Athene went from door to door
To find him comrades, for adventure's deeds.
She asked of Noemon a swift, sleek, ship;
He granted her request with ready heart,
All men and gear then needed for that trip
Were gathered, as the harbour mouth grew dark.
    Whilst to the town and suitors she brought sleep
    All the crew she led down to the beach.

24

As Boreas roared across the wine dark sea,
Telemachus then answered its loud wail
And raised a mast hewn from a young fir tree,
And made it fast with forestays; then the sail
Was hauled aloft with twisted thongs of hide;
It filled with gusts of wind as oar shafts rang
To speed the prow across each spume flecked wave,
As on she ran the curled dark waters sang.
They made all fast within the swift black ship
And set out kraters, each brim filled with wine;
They poured libations asking that their trip
Should have the blessing of the gods, divine.
 Then through the night past dawn's first light they sped
 To sandy Pylos by good fortune led.

Book 3

25

Then as the sun ascended heaven's tall heights
The ship came near to Pylos' sandy shore;
There, to the sea god bulls were sacrificed,
Nine times nine upon that beach they saw.
When all the offerings were rightly done
They moored the well built ship and furled its sail.
Athene led and told the young prince, come!
Go straight to Nestor, speak of your travail.
Unversed in subtle speech the young man stayed,
With flashing eyes the goddess urged him on—
"God favoured and well born, be undismayed,
For here news of your father must be won!"
    She led him then to where the aged king
    Sat ready with his sons to start feasting.

26

When they were seen, all thronged round, welcoming;
Peisistratus took both by the hand
And sat both down to start the revelling,
On fleeces, with his brothers, on the sand.
He served them portions of the choicest meat
Then to Athene gave a golden cup,
He told her it was Lord Poseidon's feast
And in libation turned the vessel up;
Then on the sand poured out the honeyed wine
And prayed to that great god who ruled the sea;
The goddess asked in prayer, with words divine,
For blessings on all there, and finally,
    Telemachus should find the thing he seeks:
    News of his father, mid those far off Greeks.

27

Telemachus then rose and likewise prayed
And all sat down to partake of the feast;
When satisfied Geranian Nestor made
A query: whence they came, from North or East?
Athene then put courage in the heart
Of that young lord so proudly he might ask,
And hopefully, the great king would impart
Some news which would illume the searcher's task.
The young man then revealed his lineage
And asked of those who fought and died at Troy.
The king spoke of the hero's great courage
And said: "To tell it all would years employ."
    Then looking closely at Telemachus
    Nestor saw in him: Odysseus.

28

He said in council both were of one mind,
And laid shrewd wisdom on the Argive hordes;
Odysseus' with Nestor's thoughts combined
To bring great victory to those fractious lords.
He then spoke about the quarrel which arose
When Troy lay sacked, before th' Atreides.
Then Menelaus urged that all the prows
Of their swift ships should once more breast the seas.
But Agamemnon wished all to remain
In order with rich hecatombs to please
Athene, and her dread wrath to restrain,
Yet his gesture could no god appease.
    Thus half remained and half, swift, sailed away;
    None knew then where their god-brought future lay.

29

He said: "We crossed smooth seas till reaching Tenedos,
Then, to please the gods we made a sacrifice
But Zeus then turned all golden hopes to dross,
Odysseus' ship turned back through his device."
Whilst Nestor said he fled then, sailing on,
He knew the god had evil schemes in mind,
With Diomedes, great Tydeus' son
And fair haired Menelaus just behind.
They met in Lesbos, asking there a sign
From those high gods, who gave them shrill voiced wind.
Thus swiftly blown then by that breath divine
They came to fair Geraestus as destined.
    In sacrifice for that safe journey made
    Upon the sea god's altar, bulls were laid.

30

Nestor spoke of all who came safe home,
Of Myrmidons and great Philoctetes,
Of Idomené, who safe to Crete had won,
How Agamemnon crossed those vengeful seas
And of the doom which met him on return;
And how his slayers also met their fate.
"But tidings of the rest, for which you yearn,
Are lost, from when we parted, to this date."
He hoped Telemachus would also gain
High praise from men through deeds in years to come,
The young prince prayed for strength that he regain
His lands and slay the suitors every one.
    Great Nestor said: "Odysseus though still may
    Return to make them for their insults pay."

31

Nestor said that perhaps the goddess would
Care for him as she did for his sire?
If flashing eyed Athene gave that love
For others, then may vanish all desire.
Telemachus, though thought this could not be,
He had no hope his father would return.
The goddess scolded saying destiny
Must serve her will, its power it could not spurn.
She said that grievous toil was much preferred
To swift homecoming, there by guile, to die;
As Agamemnon did while gods despaired,
For fate's decree once set none could deny.
    Telemachus though still could not believe,
    His father, lost through all those years could live.

32

Odysseus' son then turned to other things,
Enquiring how lord Agamemnon died;
With that great wisdom which long kingship brings
Nestor, son of Neleus, replied.
He told how sly Aegisthus wooed with words
Fair Clytemnestra, who in time, gave in.
Long years without a man the rogue affords
A chance to snare the best, in foulest sin.
The gods had stayed a brother's swift return:
With Menelaus home he could not risk
That murder, fearing retribution stern,
But then seduction's lust impelled the task.
    Thus in Mycenae seven rich years he reigned
    But in the eighth, Orestes vengeance gained.

33

And on that day he made the sacrifice
To celebrate his mother's just demise,
Menelaus, then through the god's device
Sailed back, beneath blue Mycenean skies.
Nestor said the lesson shown was clear
That one should never stay long from his home,
For cravens lurk with lusts subdued by fear
To take advantage, should a lord long roam.
He urged the young prince then to: "journey on
To where the fair haired Menelaus reigns.
My sons will guide you to Lacedaemon,
Your search may find reward in his domains."
 Then spoke the grey eyed goddess, thanking him
 For sacrifice, made to the great sea king.

34

Libations poured they turned to thoughts of sleep,
Beneath the stars, laid in their swift black ship;
But Nestor sought his noble guests to keep
Within his halls, in token of friendship.
Athene said Telemachus then should
Remain with him while she alone returned
Back to that vessel where his comrades stood,
Then she could give that news for which all yearned.
For like Odysseus' son they were all young
And followed him in friendship, lacking guile,
Thus she would spread encouragement among
Those men, then through night-time stay with them awhile.
 But in the morning with the rising sun
 To Cauconian lands she'd journey on.

35

Telemachus she asked, that after her
Be sent by chariot, with son as guide,
With fleetest horses swiftly yoked to bear
Him on to where they rode the eager tide.
Athene, like an eagle of the sea,
Departed and amazement fell on all,
None other than a goddess she could be;
Thus Nestor prayed for blessings on his hall.
He promised her a yearling's sacrifice,
Unbroken, with horns overlaid with gold.
In the palace wine was mixed with spice,
The wine, eleven years vintage, sweet and old.
    They drank and made libations, all his sons,
    Then well contented went back to their homes.

36

Then Nestor led the staunch young prince to sleep
On a cord bed, beneath the portico
With Peisistratus placed sharp watch to keep,
Until rose fingered dawn came creeping, low.
At first light the old king arose and went
Down to those polished stones before his door;
Sat there, long hours wise Neleus had spent
In council as Achaia's great mentor.
With sceptre held, surrounded by his heirs,
Telemachus was seated at his side,
Nestor's speech, a sacrifice prepares,
With vassals summoned there from far and wide.
    With bull brought up then for the sacred rite,
    Its horns made golden for the gods delight.

37

With water brought to purify their hands
And barley grains to sprinkle whilst in prayer
Into red flames, as ritual demands,
He cast as offering first, its new cut hair.
Thrasymedes dealt the fatal blow,
His axe sliced through the sinews of the neck,
The women's sacred wail rose from below
As black blood flowed which only death could check.
To Athene roasted thighs were laid
And of the carcass all then took repast,
Whist Polycaste, fair, the young lord bathed,
Then in bright robes she took him down at last.
    There, oil anointed, in immortal form
    He feasted well till all desire was gone.

38

Then Nestor asked his sons the car to yoke
With fine-maned horses chosen for swift pace,
With wine and dainties placed by women folk
Inside the cockpit, both then took their place.
Peisistratus drove as they set off,
With reins held tight he lightly whipped his steeds,
They sped down to the plain below Pylos;
By night they'd reached the house of Diocles.
Ortilochus's son received them well
Yet at first light they left his welcome gate,
Then through the wheat rich plain swift steeds propel
The two, to where the journey's end must wait.
    As ways grew dark with setting of the sun
    That hollow land—Lacedaemon, was won.

Book 4

39

They entered Sparta: land of dark ravines,
And drove to Menelaus' vasty hall,
Arriving there amid rich marriage scenes
With son and daughter wed mid kinfolk all.
His daughter, pledged to great Achilles' son
Would go to dwell amid the Myrmidon's,
His son had lord Alector's daughter won
And she had come to answer love's summons.
Eteoneus then saw the two arrive
And went to the high king, bearing that news;
Asking, should they stay or onwards drive
To other halls, to seek a guest friend's dues.
    The old lord called the messenger a fool
    For hosts are bound by friendship's sacred rule.

40

Reminding him how frequently had they
Been guests of others on their slow return;
These strangers thus must feast with him today:
Now welcome them, was his injunction, stern!
Eteoneus and all the other squires
Loosed their sweating horses, then with speed
Tended to their god-like guests' desires,
Whilst in their stalls the tired steeds had their feed.
When walking from the entrance to the hall
They marvelled how the high roofed palace gleamed,
For on it sun or moonbeams seemed to fall,
They gazed as round it Zeus-spilled light shafts streamed.
    Then when bathed and dressed in fine fresh robe
    They took their seats within that great abode.

41

Fair haired Menelaus greeted them
And as was custom bade them both to eat,
For asking who they were amongst all men
Could not be done till feasting was complete.
He set the fat ox chine which was his due,
Before them, as befits an honoured guest.
They ate with relish as the evening flew,
Telemachus, though, whispered a request
For Nestor's son to note the ivory,
The gleaming bronze, the silver and rare gold;
The riches in these halls and finery
Must be like those which the immortals hold.
 The old king heard his words of wonder there
 And said with Zeus no mortal could compare.

42

He told them how he brought his great wealth home
And how for eight long years he'd wandered far,
Through Cyprus and Phoenicia he did roam,
Then through Egypt led his guiding star
To Ethiopian lands, Sidonia
He met the Erembi and Lydians,
With much travail to Sparta he came near
And then returned as king, to rule his clans.
He said his wealth though brought him little joy,
With brother slain by stealth by that cursed wife
And comrades lost in that broad land of Troy,
He'd sacrifice his gold to give them life.
 He often sat mid riches ill content
 And wept for heroes, with a chill lament.

43

He told them that he mourned especially
For one who strived, enduring above all;
Whose poisoned portion, given by destiny:
Was woe, for he had vanished past recall,
And mourned he now must be by those at home,
By old Laertes and his steadfast queen,
Telemachus, the son he'd hardly known:
Odysseus that hero's name had been!
At mention of that name the young prince wept
And lifted to his eyes his purple cloak;
Menelaus saw those tears and kept
His silence, on those questions of these folk.
    Whilst he pondered thus in heart and mind
    Down came the fairest one of woman kind.

44

Like Artemis, with distaff made of gold
Came Helen, with Adraste as her maid,
Alcippe brought a soft wool rug to fold
Around her knees, whilst next to her was laid
A silver basket brought by Philo, dear,
Given by Alcandre, wife of king of Thebes:
Polybus by name who gave much gear
To Menelaus, fine wrought gifts which please.
Silver, tripods; golden talents, ten,
And to Helen too, a basket, full.
A golden distaff Phylo brought her then
So she might spin the fine dark purple wool.
    In seated comfort then she looked on all,
    And questioned those young guests within her hall.

45

She spoke of her amazement at that sight,
For there she saw Odysseus reborn,
And asked if he could be, this youthful knight,
That son he'd left now to this great hall drawn.
Menelaus with her deep thoughts concurred,
And told her of the tears that name had brought
When he to that lost hero's woes referred;
In form and gesture both were one, he'd thought.
Peisistratus then made all things clear.
Who their fathers were and why they'd come,
Then grief for loss in all brought forth a tear,
Through all that anguish which dark war had won.
 He spoke about his brother and that loss,
 Which Argives still mourn for: Antilochus!

46

With wingéd words he spoke to Menelaus
About that wisdom which the king possessed,
Old Nestor had declared: "This son of Atreus
Is in this realm, above all others blessed."
The king returned the compliment and said,
"That weeping which falls on us now should cease:
Tomorrow we will talk." And then he led
His mournful guests back to the waiting feast.
A squire poured cleansing water on their hands
And Helen cast a drug into their wine
Which lifted pain and strife, with which it stands
To give, a while, forgetfulness divine.
 From Egypt she'd obtained this subtle gift
 Which Thon's wife told her would crushed spirits, lift.

47

Then Helen told the tale of how in Troy,
Odysseus came in a low slave's disguise,
Within its walls to spy, a reckless ploy!
To gauge its strength, its legions to apprise.
She alone amongst them realised
Who that man was and sought to question him;
Bathing him, he could not stay disguised,
Anointing him she knew each noble limb.
But there he made her swear a mighty oath
Not to make him known amid his foes;
When she'd sworn he told her all the truth
Of why Greece came, increasing Troy's dark woes.
    He then returned to bring his captains word
    And going back killed many with his sword.

48

The Spartan woman wept but she was glad,
Alone in Troy yet thinking of her home;
At love's deluding blindness she grew sad,
For child and bridal chamber left alone.
Then Menelaus spoke of later times
With all those captains in the wooden horse,
Brought into Troy within its dark confines,
And how she'd come into its main concourse.
She probed the wooden beast then slowly, thrice,
Circled round it speaking with each voice
Of wives of all those hid in that device;
Those sounds in turn made each lord's heart rejoice.
    Each wished to rise and leave and make reply,
    One lord alone made each his wish, deny.

49

By doing that Odysseus saved them all
And then Athene led the maid away;
The king said now let sleep come to this hall
We all need rest till woken by new day.
Menelaus then rose at early dawn
And sought out the young prince and asked him why
Across the foam flecked sea swift sails had bourn
Him to the Spartan lands, his quest to try.
Telemachus then told him of his plight
And how his house was brought near ruin, by greed;
He sought news of his father so he might
Mourn him, or return with vengeful speed.
    The great king cursed at what those vile men dared
    And hoped a day would come when none were spared.

50

He prayed to all the gods he might return
To that strength of youth, when once arose
And with a prince of Lesbos took his turn
In wrestling, winning with his skilful throws.
Then in response to that which was beseeched,
He spoke about the old man of the sea;
To Pharos harbour then his journey'd reached,
He lay becalmed by some cruel destiny.
Till wandering round the isle he came upon
Eidothea (her father: Proteus);
She asked him why he lingered there so long
He said fate held him there: the will of Zeus!
    In pity then she told him of that one
    Her sire, the vassal of Poseidon.

51

That old man of the sea knew all its deeps
And often came to this place where they spoke,
"If you can catch him where the white surf leaps
He must tell you how to reach your folk.
At mid-day he will come bourn by the wind,
Hid by the blue-dark ripples of the tide,
In hollow caves there sleeping you will find
Him laid among those seals, who with him ride."
She said at dawn that she would take him there
With three companions, strong, to lie in wait
But of his crafty wiles she warned: beware!
If caught he would try hard to change his shape.
 "At length though when he speaks in changing form
 He must then your dearest wish, perform."

52

As dawn appeared we went down to the sea,
While from its depths she brought out seal skins, four.
We lay while from their stench she made us free
With sweet Ambrosia smeared round face and jaw.
His seals came forth in throngs as she had said
And at full noon old Proteus emerged,
He counted till content then took his bed,
Then with a shout upon him we all surged
To grasp him firm, and hold unflinchingly;
We saw him first into a Lion turn,
A serpent, then a leopard we did see,
A huge boar, then a rapid flowing burn.
 Finally, a high and leafy tree
 But we held on and he could not break free.

53

The old man spoke, enquiring of their need
And ask which god had told them: "Catch him there!"
Then Proteus said: "to Egypt you must lead
Your men and a great sacrifice prepare.
When holy hecatombs are offered, then
The gods will grant the journey you desire."
The king agreed once more with ship and men
To make that weary voyage, long and dire.
He asked the sea god of those left at Troy
Whom he and Nestor last saw long ago;
Proteus, with dark words, gave little joy
And said: "Now most in Hades dwell below!
    The chieftains, all but one, the gods had damned
    And he still wandered in some far off land."

54

Aias was lost amid his long oared ships,
Through hubris, as he gained land he was cursed,
Near Gyraes rocks these proud words left his lips:
"In spite of all the gods the sea's he'd worsed."
Poseidon heard his boastful voice and so
Took up his trident in his mighty hands,
And smote the rock, which shattered, thus below
Drowned in boundless deeps that hero ends.
He then recalled great Agamemnon's fate,
Who came safe home, to die through treachery.
Then last of all he went on to relate
Of one alone who'd come safe from the sea:
    Odysseus, who on Calypso's isle
    Remained in sorrow, captive to her guile.

55

The old man, of his captor's ending spoke,
That he should not succumb as other men:
To death! Conveyed to Hades in its yoke,
But to Elysian fields must journey when
Fair haired Rhadamanthus so ordained.
As husband to the daughter of great Zeus
From Helen was this final gift obtained;
After this the old man was let loose.
Then Proteus plunged beneath the surging sea,
And Menelaus, broodingly, returned
Back to his ships to ponder destiny,
And through immortal night for home to yearn.
But first a journey on the grey sea waits
And sacrifice as ordained by the fates.

56

Thus back to Egypt and the heaven fed Nile
To offer up the perfect hecatombs;
Thus propitiated must the gods resile
From vengeance, which that journey back foredooms.
Before he left he heaped up a great mound
In memory of great Agamemnon's name;
That his deeds would ever be renowned,
Unquenchable for ever be his fame.
After this the gods sent winds so fair
That swiftly he regained his native land.
There Menelaus bade the young lords share
His treasures; then to journey on as planned.
But Telemachus chaffed at the delay
And eager still for news would leave next day.

57

Great Menelaus knew that duty urged
The young man on his quest, thus as a gift,
A bowl he offered, which Hephastus forged,
Then once more turned to feast before he left.
Meanwhile on Ithaca the suitors met
And sported, for then most were unaware,
That the young prince on the last tide had left
For Pylos, seeking news in his despair.
From Noemon he'd taken a black ship,
Antinous asked then who his comrades were;
Then learning of that noble comradeship
Raged hard, that this, Odysseus' son should dare.
 He sought at once a vessel to pursue
 The young lord, with a vile and vengeful crew.

58

Penelope knew of the suitors schemes,
The herald Medon heard them, standing near,
And told her they would slay her son it seems,
For of his quest's success they stood in fear.
Soul consuming grief fell on the queen
And at her chamber's threshold then she swooned:
Would great Odysseus never more be seen?
And was the son she bore him also doomed?
For he had vanished on the storm swept seas,
Without her knowledge, venturing abroad.
In anguish she bewailed those destinies
Which captured both her son, and noble lord.
 She sent for aged Dolius to go
 And tell Laertes of her black sorrow.

59

Eurycleia spoke then of her oath:
That she would hold her tongue for twelve long days!
She'd kept the secret of the journey both
And stores, provided for those salt sea ways.
She told the Queen to bathe and then to pray
To great Athene for his safe return;
This stopped the weeping, ended that dismay
Which filled her thoughts, of what those deeds might earn.
She offered barley, raised the sacred cry,
Up to the goddess asking her for aid;
Athene heard her, then could not deny
That request which her depth of need had made.
    High from her chamber, cries the suitors heard
    And thought at last for marriage she'd prepared.

60

They knew that death was mooted for her son
But none knew how to actuate their plot,
Antinous said that: "this needs to be done
With caution, twenty men we should allot
To man a ship, we need the very best."
With all agreed, the murderers embarked.
Meanwhile the Queen, at home, could take no rest
For fear that her dear son for death was marked.
Athene thought to send a comforter
Thus, as Ipthime, sent a phantom form,
In dreams it said: "the burden that you bear
Will melt to nothing with the coming dawn.
    Your son will come safe home, that is assured,
    The goddess guides him till his ship is moored."

61

Penelope then asked about her lord:
The man of many sorrows, gone so long;
The shadowed phantom would not speak the word
Which said he lived, or had to Hades gone.
The phantom glided through the open door
And then into the swift breath of the wind;
The Queen awoke, heart warmed from what she saw,
For fears of day sweet dreams of night rescind.
With utter murder in their evil hearts
The suitors sailed across the ocean ways.
For Asteris' small isle their ship departs
To lie in ambush mid its hidden bays.
  Near rugged Samos, filled with lust and hate,
  They hoped with blood their greed born thirsts to sate.

Book 5

62

Now from her couch arose new waking dawn,
Leaving lord Tithonous there once more,
For she must always leave with waking morn
To bring first light to hill, and vale and shore.
Athene to the gods recalled those woes
Which lord Odysseus so long had to bear;
Shipwrecked abroad, at home beset by foes,
And languishing in fair Calypso's lair.
Zeus, replying, said that she should guide
Telemachus back to his home unharmed;
He then called loyal Hermes to his side,
To send him where that nymph too long had charmed
    That man of many sorrows in her bed,
    In hope to win his love that they might wed.

63

Zeus then said Calypso must be told
That she should let Odysseus go free,
Then he could build a raft, with purpose bold,
And then set out upon the storm wracked sea.
For twenty days, in peril, he must drift
Until he reached rich Sheria's safe shore,
Phaeacians there would generously gift
Him ship and gold and other gifts; far more
Than those in Troy he could have gained.
Then Hermes bound his golden sandals on,
Those which bore him like the winds, unchained,
For now the god-kings bidding must be done.
    He took the wand which lulls all men to sleep,
    Or bids them wake and dreamed commandments keep.

64

At Pieria he stepped down from the air
To cross the sea's huge gulfs and mighty heights,
He reached the cave which was Calypso's lair
And stood and marvelled at the isle's delights.
For round about a fragrant wood grove grew
Of poplars, elders and sweet cypresses,
There nested owls and falcons, sea-crows too,
Which ply their business on the violet seas.
By her hollow cave and trailing vine
And watered by four springs: a meadow sweet,
With blooms, vine clusters, full and in their prime,
All who came this gorgeous sight did greet.
    Herself, sat singing, at the golden loom;
    A fire of fragrant cedar lit the gloom.

65

Great Odysseus though was not within
For he sat weeping on the barren shore,
Calypso greeted Hermes, welcoming,
And sat him down and asked what news he bore,
But first gave him ambrosia to eat
And mixed red nectar so the god might drink,
Then when his heart was satisfied, replete,
She said now of the mortal she must think,
For Zeus now wished the wretched man should leave,
For too long had he suffered far from home.
At these words her heart began to grieve,
That she should lose the one claimed as her own.
    She asked which envy caused the gods to hate
    Those men with whom immortals sought to mate.

66

When rosy fingered Dawn chose Orion
He was assailed by Artemis, with darts;
When Demeter lay down to love Iasion
Zeus then killed him with his deadly arts,
And with his lightning he had likewise struck
That ship which bore Odysseus and crew;
He alone I rescued from that wreck
And found that love, which now my heart must rue.
Lord Zeus commands, I cannot disobey,
I have no ships but I will urge him on.
The goddess found him weeping near the bay
And bade him leave and said what must be done.
    She told him with his axe to hew down trees
    And make a raft; then launch it on the seas.

67

She promised him provisions and a wind
To blow him back towards his native land,
And said his journey there was god destined;
He asked the Nymph, if mischief she had planned?
Calypso stroked him with her hand and smiled,
Upbraiding him, for words of roguish wit.
She made that oath which may not be defiled,
By Heaven and Earth and Styx and swore on it,
That she would do her best to see him home,
And then he followed to her hollow cave;
They feasted long, and when all there was done,
She asked what deep desire could make him leave,
    Enquiring if beside Penelope
    She was worse in looks by some degree?

68

He said his wife was mortal, and in looks
No match for one who time could never age,
Though how he longed for Ithaca's sweet brooks
To get back home he'd risk the wild sea's rage,
And that of any god who sought to smite
Him as he toiled to cross the wine dark sea,
Though once again his journey home would blight
Him with those sorrows: his, by fates decree.
For one last time the two made love till dawn;
Then dressed in white and gold, her beauty veiled,
She brought him tools to build, as he had sworn
A raft of timbers hewn and well trenailed.
    He set a mast and yard and at the rear
    Mounted a long oar, with which to steer.

69

The fourth day came and all his work was done,
And on the fifth she sent him on his way,
In fragrant clothing of the fine yarn spun,
Well provisioned then, without delay.
Odysseus spread his sail to catch the breeze
And plied the steering oar with captain's skill;
He did not sleep but watched the Pleiades
And other forms, which star point legends fill.
For seventeen days then guided by his star
He sailed and on the eighteenth, nearing land
Saw shadow shapes of mountains from afar;
That kingdom, which Phaeacian chiefs command.
    But lord Poseidon saw him from the height
    Of Solymi, where peak and cloud unite.

70

In anger that the gods had let him sail
He vowed to bring down evil on that head;
He seized his trident, roused a mighty gale,
And from fair calms such angry storm seas bred.
East and west and north and south winds clashed,
In fury, raising up a mighty wave,
Which, angrily, around Odysseus thrashed;
He thought those briny depths would be his grave.
Bemoaning fate he wished he'd died in Troy—
There laid to rest with funeral rites, in fame,
Now here, alone, wild seas would soon destroy
His raft, and he would drown unknown by name.
  His mast was shattered by the fierce storm blast,
  And he was on those churning waters cast.

71

A great wave overwhelmed him with its might,
And by wet clothes, weighed down, he could not rise;
At last, he struggled up into the light
And swam to where he'd seen his raft capsize.
He spat out bitter brine but fate was kind,
He reached the wreck and once more climbed aboard,
And sitting at its centre hoped to find
Escape from doom amid that storm's discord.
The four winds flung it on the heaving swell
Like thistle tufts blown round the autumn plain,
Till Ino saw him in that salt pell-mell,
And taking pity rose up from the main.
  There in a sea-mew's form she spoke to him
  To tell him how the dry shore he might win.

72

Poseidon though had willed him ceaseless pain,
Thus he must strip his clothes and leave the raft
And try by swimming dry land to regain.
The goddess gave a god-spun veil as gift
And said its spells would save him from all harm,
But once ashore the veil he must return
Back to the wine dark sea, thrown by his arm;
Then from the sea god's kingdom he must turn.
She went to leave and plunged into the waves
Whilst he, perplexed, long pondered on her words,
He thought to cling still to the raft's stout staves,
Until the tempest cast him from its boards.
 He saw a mountain wave above him come;
 His refuge wrecked by angry Poseidon.

73

Odysseus rode a plank like some sea horse
And stripped his garments, fastening the veil
Beneath his breast, he braved the torrents force,
Then Poseidon knew he must prevail
And left him to his sea-whipped suffering.
Then fair Athene roused the northern wind
And bade the others cease that it might bring
Him, three days hence, to the Phaeacian land.
In sight of it a great wave raised him up
And swept him, swimming, to the welcome shore,
In sight of safety came the bitter cup:
He heard wild waves against a sharp reef roar.
 And nowhere could he see smooth sand which might
 Permit him to escape his god-cursed plight.

74

In peril there Athene spurred him on,
And made him think to swim beyond that rage
To find a place to put his foot upon,
That from the watery grave he might resurge.
He found a river, to its god he prayed,
For there no rock, or reef stood in his way,
The current ceased, he saw the billows fade,
And safe at last he staggered from the bay.
He lay exhausted there, flesh bruised and torn,
But on reviving thought about the veil
And there released the gift which he had worn,
Without it may have ended all travail.
    A great wave bore it seawards from the sands
    Then Ino once more took it in her hands.

75

Odysseus then amid the reeds sank down
And kissed the earth which yields up grain to men;
For stranded, naked, far from any town
He sought a place to rest in safety then.
He crept between two bushes, one a thorn
And one an olive, shaded from the sun;
In shelter from the bitter winds and storm
He needed rest, his sea-torn trials were done.
To make a soft bed there he swept up leaves,
Which lay in heaped profusion all around,
There in that coverlet which autumn weaves
He laid himself to rest down on the ground.
    Athene gave sleep's gift with her caress
    To free him from his toil-born weariness.

Book 6

76

Now while the much enduring hero slept
Athene went to the Phaeacian land,
And into Nausicaa's night chamber swept,
And while she dreamt gave her this strong command:
That they must launder clothes at break of day,
As Dymas' daughter she had taken form,
Complaining her bright clothes now scattered lay,
Thus she must ask her father after dawn
To ready mules and wagon with all speed,
So she could take her garments there to clean
Them at the river where pure streamlets feed
Those washing tanks, where clothes were made pristine.
    At sunrise then with all sweet sleep dispelled
    She went to do what her strange dream compelled.

77

Alcinous agreed to her request,
For mules and sturdy wagons to convey
Her to the river side, with maidens, lest
Her fine things should stay soiled another day.
Her mother gave her dainties and sweet wine
And oil, from olives, in a flask of gold
With all things ready for the bright shoreline
Nausicaa, of whip and reins, took hold.
They went down to the river's sparkling streams,
Which feed the washing tanks and never fails,
There water in abundance falls and cleans;
Its ceaseless flow no summer drought curtails.
    They trampled dirt stained garments in those tanks,
    Then laid them out to dry on shingle banks.

78

They bathed and dined then fell to playing ball,
And Nausicaa above all others shone,
Like Artemis amid those wood nymphs, tall,
Who hunt with her and after wild boar run.
The orb was thrown and landed in the sea
This caused them all to cry aloud, dismayed.
Odysseus, waking, looked out cautiously
To where those fair tressed women sang and played.
Though naked he came forth to face those maids,
Yet broke a leafy branch to hide his shame,
And like some lion from dark wooded glades
Onto the shore with blazing eyes he came.
    All fled that creature, wild and caked in brine,
    Apart from one emboldened maid, divine.

79

Athene lifted from the maid her fear,
Thus Nausicaa, alone, to face him stayed.
Odysseus thought it best not to come near
But from a distance, cautious greeting made.
With winning words which flattered her he asked:
Was she a goddess, or could mortal be?
He said her form such shining beauty masked,
Which in earth born maids was rare to see.
He told her from Ogygia he'd come,
Adrift for twenty days upon the sea,
By fate's command from peril's heart he'd won
His way to shore, placed there by destiny.
    He asked her to have pity on his plight
    And for some rag to clothe a shipwrecked wight.

80

Then Nausicaa, the white armed, understood;
Before her was no ordinary man,
She gave him garments, saying soon she would
Take him home to meet her noble clan,
And spoke to him about her father dear:
Alcinous, of all the people: king.
She called her maidens, who still hid in fear,
And ordered them sweet wine and food to bring,
And then to bathe him in that sheltered spot
At which the sheltered river felt no wind.
Odysseus begged them: "stay beyond eyeshot,
To save my naked shame from woman kind!"
    He washed caked brine away from shoulders broad,
    And from surf tangled hair, till well restored.

81

He clothed, his skin made smooth with shining oil,
And sly Athene filled his form with grace
And beauty, which no mortal form could spoil;
His hair hung curled and light shone from his face.
Nausicaa now thought the gods had sent
This vision there, the man that she desired,
Her future husband, she felt well content
For in her heart deep need and hope conspired.
She ordered all her maids to bring him food,
And drink, which he devoured there ravenously;
For days devoid of sustenance he'd stood:
Adrift, bourn by the wild and empty sea.
    When satiated, then the princess spoke
    And told him of the customs of her folk.

82

She said that they were bondsmen of the waves,
That all were called as crew to sail some ship
To work on canvas, cables, shaping staves
To form thin oar blades, ready for some trip.
In fear of gossip from the common sort
She begged Odysseus follow her and wait,
If he was seen beside her as escort,
She would endure reproof or vile debate.
Thus he followed, as back home she drove,
And at the city's outskirts left him there,
To wait in great Athene's sacred grove;
He sat in hope and offered up a prayer.
    That by Phaeacia's king he be received
    And welcomed as a guest friend in great need.

Book 7

83

The maiden reached her father's palace gate,
And crowding round, her splendid brothers came.
They unhitched mules and saw to all her freight;
She went inside and found that aged dame:
Eurymedusa, brought from Apeire,
And as a gift presented to the king;
She had nursed his daughter from that day
Serving food, and new fires kindling.
As instructed, now that she was home,
Odysseus followed to the city walls,
Athene poured thick mist that he might come
Unrecognised, towards Phaecian halls.
    The goddess met him as a maiden dressed,
    Then at the gate his purpose he confessed.

84

He said he sought to find Alcinous,
Lord of that city and its people, rare,
For as a stranger here he must discuss
The voyage home, to end his long despair.
The goddess told Odysseus: "take heed
And walk in silence and avoid all eyes,"
Then through the people she could safely lead
Him to the palace, needing no disguise.
Athene took him through her shielding mists,
Thus no Phaeacian noticed as they passed,
With pathways veiled and covered in its drifts
They walked and reached the palace doors at last.
    The goddess said: "within you'll find the king,
    His noble aid may end your wandering."

85

Athene left him at the threshold then,
Odysseus marvelled there at what he saw:
Silver doorposts, and attached to them
Of fine wrought gold, was made each splendid door.
The walls were bronze, above them cyanus
Was set at cornice, shining brilliant blue;
Either side stood dogs which Hepheastus
Had fashioned, made of gold and silver too.
Inside fine seats were fixed along each wall,
Each decorated with soft fabric drapes;
Phaeacian traders ate within the hall
Of finest foods, with wine from choicest grapes.
    On pedestals stood golden youths—at night
    Their torches filled that dining space with light.

86

Fifty women milled the yellow grain,
Whilst others wove soft yarn or worked the loom,
Orchards grew outside that rich domain
Where fruit grew ripe each day, in luscious bloom.
Pomegranates pears and figs were found,
Grapes and apples, olives bloomed all year;
Springs arose to irrigate the ground
And warm west winds brought never ceasing cheer.
Yet after he had drunk these marvels in
Odysseus went in the splendid hall,
He saw Phaeacia's nobles and their king,
A cloud of mist still hid him from them all.
    When he reached Arête, who was queen,
    The veil of mist dissolved and he was seen.

87

He grasped Arête's knees and made his prayer
As supplicant, and told her of his plight;
All marvelled seeing such a man come there,
Silence fell among them at that sight.
He pleaded, that one born of Rhexenor
Would give him speedy means to travel home;
And said how he had suffered since Troy's war,
By malign fate forever forced to roam.
He sat down in the ashes by the fire,
And then among them spoke Eceneus,
With wisdom saying: "sure the kings desire
Could not be long to leave the stranger thus!"
    Alcinous then raised Odysseus up
    And sat him near so he might drink and sup.

88

A golden pitcher, filled with water clear,
Was poured into a bowl, of silver made;
Odysseus washed his hands then took his cheer
From that abundance now before him laid.
The king then told his heralds: "serve the wine!"
That all to Zeus might a libation pour.
All drank their fill until late evening time
Then for home readied at the palace door.
Alcinous said: when the morning came
He would summon all the elders there,
To think how this strange man might home shores gain
And all things needful for his trip prepare.
    He wondered if the gods had formed some plan
    Who'd come to test them, flesh clothed, as a man.

89

Odysseus assured them he was none
Else than mortal, sadly bound to age,
And said through many sorrows he had won
To reached their shore wrecked by the sea god's rage.
His anguish made him hungry thus he asked
That he might eat, and through that joy forget,
Requesting: when dawn came these men be tasked
To send him home, and end long years regret.
They praised his words then each went to his home
And he was left, sat with the king and queen;
Arête asked him how he came to roam
And who he was, and where his land had been.
    She recognised the finery he wore
    And asked how he had come by them, therefore.

90

Odysseus told her of his journey there
And how he met sweet maidens on the shore;
Then how their daughter gave him clothes to wear
And lead him, hidden, to the palace door.
Alcinous said: "straightway to his halls,
By Nausicaa, he should have been conveyed;"
Odysseus replied: "that no blame falls
Upon her head, on mine it should be laid."
The king saw godly virtue in this man
And said that if he chose with them to stay
As husband for his daughter, as his son,
Wealth and honour would that act repay.
    Yet no such gifts could keep him from his home,
    Their ships must bear him through the high sea foam.

91

The king spoke of the prowess of his men,
Whom Rhadamanthus to Euboea bore,
And effortless returned that day again
From that son of Earth's most distant shore.
He then saw that Odysseus must rest
And ordered sleep until the morning came;
That voyager was glad and on Zeus pressed
A prayer, that the high king should gain great fame.
Arête told her maids to place a bed,
With purple drapes beneath the portico,
And over these warm fleeces they should spread
So he could soundly sleep without sorrow.
    Then to their chamber king and queen retired,
    All things there being done, as they desired.

Book 8

92

Alcinous arose with early dawn
To lead the way to where all elders meet,
And with him, too, Odysseus, Zeus born,
Each went down and sat on his stone seat.
Athene, as a herald, roamed abroad
And called all down to see the stranger there;
She told them, as a god appeared that lord,
A wonder to behold; beyond compare.
Many came and looked on him with awe,
The goddess having filled his form with grace,
That he may win them as he stood before
Their noble nation at its meeting place.
    The king then urged that they should choose a ship
    With two and fifty youths, with oars for it.

93

Alcinous made invite to his halls
Whilst all was readied for the restless sea,
He summoned then to sing within his walls
Demodocus, divine in minstrelsy.
The palace filled with men of all degrees;
A feast for all who came, prepared the king,
With oxen, sheep and boars, picked out to please;
All gathered there then saw the herald bring
That minstrel loved above all by the muse,
Who good and evil on him had bestowed:
She'd gifted song yet caused him, sight, to lose,
Thus from his lyre the sweetest music flowed.
    Placed in their midst sat in a silver chair
    They feasted him till all were sated there.

94

The muse then moved the minstrels heart to sing
Of deeds of famous men, which led to war;
Of lord Odysseus and that quarrelling
With great Achilles, leading to Troy's door.
Odysseus heard the minstrel's song and groaned,
And draped his purple cloak about his head,
For shame, for tears fell as he grieving moaned
With thoughts of those past deeds and heroes dead.
Alcinous alone saw how he wept
Each time the lyre struck notes ran through the hall;
Thus all the nobles from that feast he swept
To start those doughty games, which test men all.
    Their finest youth rose ready to compete
    In trials which strength could win, or swiftest feet.

95

Clytoneus, son of Alcinous
In racing was the fleetest youth by far.
In wrestling none could match Euryalus,
The peer of Ares, mighty god of war.
With discus furthest thrown by Elatreus
And in boxing Laodamus won,
In jumping none could beat Amphialus,
All hearts took pleasure in what there was done.
Amongst the victors, asked Laodamus
If with them there the stranger would take part,
For by his build he thought Odysseus
Could prove their rival in each skilful art.
    But low in spirit there, the lord replied
    And chidingly, that challenge put, denied.

96

Euryalus with barbéd taunts then said:
"That he looked like a captain bound by greed
And not like one who was to contests bred,
Who nurtured gain far more than honour's need."
With anger hard Odysseus answered him:
"That gods made choices with their bounteous gifts
To one denied good looks or grace of limb
They beauty gave to words breathed from their lips."
He said that youth was given a godlike look
Yet by his insults showed a lowly mind,
Though weary from his toils he would not brook
Such imputations from one of his kind.
    Thus up he leapt and seized a discus huge
    That he might there his godlike prowess prove.

97

He spun and from his hand the stone leapt forth
To hum in flight and land past all their marks,
In man-form there, Athene marked its worth
And he rejoiced on hearing her remarks.
With lighter heart Odysseus challenged them
To every form of contest in the games;
Athene spoke for all Phaeacian men
To soothe his heart, and damp his anger's flames.
The goddess said that now was time to dance
And drink the music of the hollow lyre
To clear the ring and let our youth advance
With nimble feet, to tread the golden gyre.
    Demodocus was brought back to their midst,
    And sweetest chords there played that rhapsodist.

98

He sang the song of love between those two
Fair Aphrodite and the god of war:
Great Ares, who in secret came to woo
And lay with her behind her husband's door.
But Helios observed that shame filled deed
And went to tell Hephaestus he was wronged;
The smith in anger went away to feed
His forge, till flames around the red iron thronged.
On his great anvil then he forged those bands
Which neither god nor man could loose or break;
Then in his chamber with his mighty hands
He fixed them round the bed, that pair to take,
  When ever vile seduction should begin
  And trap the two in shame, in midst of sin.

99

The bonds were spun, as spider's webs so fine
That none could see them hanging from the beams,
Thus when vile Ares sought that couch divine,
A god-wrought snare would end those love drenched dreams.
Hephaestus made as though he would depart
To Lemnes, and the war god saw him go
Thus hurried, hot with lust, to win the heart
Once more of she who waited, weak, below.
He urged his lover quickly into bed
And fairest Cytherea did not demur,
Thus to love's couch she readily was led:
Sweet pangs of rapture, eager to endure.
  As they lay down the bonds about them fell;
  Which sly Hephaestus' skill had forged so well.

100

With limbs bound tightly neither could escape,
And now the lame god angrily returned,
Crying he was scorned through his mis-shape,
For fires of grief and anger in him burned.
He said they would stay bound till Zeus repaid
Those gifts of wooing for his daughters shame;
He called on all the gods to see them laid
On their adulterous bed, in guilt's red shame.
The gods all gathered at the great bronze doors
And roared with laughter at Hephaestus' guile;
No goddess came, for there the marriage laws
Lay broken and must all their kind defile.
    The lame had caught the swift, despite his speed;
    The gods thought him well punished for his deed.

101

But great Apollo saw another side
And asked Lord Hermes if he too would lie
With that seductress, though another's bride,
To taste sweet pleasures drowned in ecstasy.
Argeiphontes answered, saying yes:
He would suffer shame and thrice those bonds
That beauty: Aphrodite, to possess,
To feel that rapture of love's harsh commands.
His words raised ribald laughter from the gods
But lord Poseidon, bearer of the earth,
With all that shameful humour was at odds,
For he alone saw danger in their mirth.
    He begged Hephaestus: "set lord Ares free!"
    Thus, he could then pay back the wedding fee.

102

Hephaestus was not keen for surety
From such a rascal as the god there bound;
Poseidon vowed that in entirety,
It would be paid, and from him could be found.
The lame god said he could not now refuse
And freed the chains that bound the two in shame;
They sprang apart now that the bonds were loose
And both sped off, too sin-stained to remain.
Ares went to Thrace to sulk and fret
But Aphrodite, to be purified,
Went to Phapos where the Graces kept
Those sacred oils which cleansed and sanctified.
  They bathed her, thus contently she laid
  Restored in beauty, goldenly arrayed.

103

This was the song the famous minstrel sang,
And all were glad who listened to his words;
Then to the dance floor Laodamus sprang
With Halius as best of all those lords,
In leaping as they caught the purple ball,
Thrown up high towards the shade filled cloud,
They danced and threw with time then beat by all
And at the end applause came long and loud.
Odysseus spoke then to the noble king
To compliment him on the dancer's skill;
Alcinous let words of friendship ring
Throughout his hall with pleasure and goodwill
  And pride to hear the noble stranger's praise,
  A gift then in return he sought to raise.

104

A cloak, a tunic and a piece of gold
He asked from all Phaeacia's thirteen kings
As fitting for that stranger in their fold;
Euryalus for his well shamed slightings
He asked to make amends and so decree:
The young man said a bronze sword would he give
With silver hilt, and scabbard—ivory,
And ask their lordly guest there to forgive.
Odysseus nobly answered him and prayed
The gods would grant long joy to that young squire;
At sunset with those gifts before him laid
A great feast waited, then he could retire.
    The lordly heralds led him to the hall
    With gifts to show to the Phaeacian's all.

105

Before the queen the shining gifts were laid.
Alcinous said: "bring your finest chest
For there will lie this finery displayed,
With cloak and tunic, chosen from your best."
He ordered then a cauldron to be placed
Upon the fire so that their guest could bathe,
Thus kindling wood beneath the iron was spaced
Then flames rose up, its belly to enswathe.
Alcinous brought out a cup of gold
To give his guest for use in future years,
So he would think then of those days of old
With pleasure at the end of all his cares.
    With all performed as ordered by the king
    Odysseus went to join the revelling.

106

Nausicaa, with graceful beauty blessed,
Stood by the doorpost of the well built hall
And marvelled as her gazing eyes possessed
God-like Odysseus standing, handsome, tall.
She spoke regretful words of sad farewell
And said: "back in your land, remember me
I gave you life, that far off you may dwell,
This is your fate, decreed by destiny."
He said: "that on returning on all days
That he would pray to her in gratitude,
Set as a goddess, hymned by golden lays
For her great gifts, amid this plenitude."
 He then sat down next to Alcinous
 The herald then led in Demodocus.

107

The minstrel, held in honour by them all
Was seated in their midst, prepared to sing,
The herald first was summoned by the call
Of their great guest who gave him meat to bring:
That finest portion of the white tusked boar,
To that blind singer as his fair greeting;
The herald took the gift across the floor,
Then all joined in, in cheerful banqueting.
When all were done Odysseus made request,
That songs were sung about the wooden horse,
And of the guile which led to Troy's conquest,
By passing walls, which ten years failed to force.
 Unfortunate that choice, then one of three,
 Which Priam's people made at fate's decree.

108

Some wished to cleave those timbers with the bronze
Whilst others sought to cast it from high rocks,
But most of those beguiled Dardanian sons
Made that choice which Hades' gates unlocks,
Bringing it inside, to propitiate
The gods: they thought the Argives all had gone!
At night the Greeks poured forth and sealed the fate
Of Ilium—thereby the war was won.
This was the song the famous minstrel sang,
Yet hearing it, Odysseus wept salt tears
And piteous groans from deep within him sprang
As memories of death rose from past years.
    He fought to hide his grief for all those slain,
    Alcinous alone knew of his pain.

109

He spoke among those lovers of the oar
And asked the minstrel to set down his lyre;
He told them of the burden their guest bore,
How grief and sorrow bound his heart entire.
That as a brother he had been received
Amongst them all with gifts and friendships dear;
He asked him then, so none could be deceived,
To speak out his own name there, loud and clear.
To tell of antecedents and his home
And where he'd wandered on his journey, long,
And of those peoples found as he did roam
And why Troy's doom hot tears from him had wrung.
    He asked if kin had died at Ilium
    And what sorrow caused such grief to come?

Book 9

110

Odysseus to his great host replied:
"Alcinous, renowned above all men,
When minstrels sing it cannot be denied,
Great pleasure comes upon the people then;
But you have asked me of my grievous woes,
Those which now still make me weep and groan;
In uncounted numbers these arose
And through long years they've kept me from my home."
He gave his name to all assembled there
And told them of his home isle: "Ithaca"!
Of its forest slopes and mountain bare
Call Neriton which all could see afar.
 "Near it Dulchium and Same lie
 With Zachinthus' wooded Isle nearby."

111

He said that: "Ithaca lies furthest west
Of all the isles, and lowest in the sea;
Its rugged slopes among these were the best
And for its men a good nurse thought to be.
Though Circe held him sometime in her halls,
And fair Calypso in her hollow caves,
Their charms could never drown his home isle's calls,
And still for those sweet shores a sad heart craves."
He then described his journey home from Troy,
Firstly speaking of the Cicones,
Who they attacked, a city to destroy,
And women to enslave and treasure seize.
 With all that done he urged them: share the spoils!
 Then leave with haste from those forbidding shores.

112

But folly ruled and all ignored his plea,
With sheep and cattle slaughtered by the shore,
They drank and feasted, slaves to destiny,
Meanwhile Cicones gathered more and more
Of their best fighters from adjacent lands,
And line of battle by the swift ships formed.
While day was waxing all attacking bands
Were beaten back and a brief respite earned,
But at its waning then death's work was done
And six Achaians perished from each ship,
Those who survived, before they journeyed on
Let cries of grief rush out between each lip.
    Zeus then roused the North wind: tempest strong,
    Which ripped their sales and drove each ship along.

113

The sails were dropped and stowed for fear of death
Then all hands rowed the ships toward the land;
For two long days they braved the storm's harsh breath,
For two long nights the groaning oars were manned.
When fair tressed Dawn gave birth to the third day
Those winds abated, then canvas was set
To sweep their ships across those waters grey,
But waves and currents drove them backward yet;
Round the isle of Malee led their sails,
Then past Cythera their ship was driven;
For nine long days they fled before the gales
Till Boreas' great strength began to slacken.
    Thus on the tenth day land at last was reached,
    With masts let down then all the ships were beached.

114

Within that land the Lotus-eaters dwelled,
Who take a flowery food, and life forget;
We ate and drank, then with our hunger quelled
Sent out three companions, brave, to get
Some knowledge of the people of that place.
They found those souls who lived on that strange food,
These gave my men the Lotus fruit to taste,
It bound them to its dreams in servitude,
For they no longer wished then to return
But longed to stay, with thoughts of home excised.
They always for its honeyed sweetness yearned,
And wept when its addiction was denied.
    For they were dragged back, bound, and placed beneath
    The benches of our ship, with no relief.

115

I bade my trusty crew to seek the seas;
Hence on we sailed, though grieving in our hearts.
We came unto the land of Cyclopes,
A wild and lawless clan born of those parts.
They neither sow nor plant the fertile land,
Despite this, in profusion, all things grow:
Fruitful vines and wheat and barley stand
In fields of plenty, all without the plough.
They have no laws and councils do not need
And dwell on mountain peaks in hollow caves;
For separate lives their, man ruled, families lead,
Concerned with their small space, with no conclave.
    Nearby an island stands where wild goats breed,
    No hunters come while on its slopes they feed.

116

The Cyclopes possess no red prowed ships,
No craftsmen who could build them for the sea,
They have no use for trading or those trips
To distant isles, across the waters free.
A harbour there provides safe anchorage
With no stern cables or ropes at the fore;
When we arrived there was no light to gauge
Our way but through some god we reached the shore.
There we disembarked and fell asleep
Till wakened by the rosy fingered dawn;
We roamed the island, saw the wild goats leap
And then took up the bow to hunt that morn.
    Abundant prey then fell to every crew
    Which feasted there until night's shadows grew.

117

Well fed with meat, replete with sweet red wine,
We once more rested on the golden strand,
But when Dawn lit that land a second time
I called the crews and gave them my command:
That all should stay except my ship and crew,
For we would leave to learn more of these men
And row to where those dwellings we could view;
To find if they were kind or wild, and then
We went on board and rapidly embarked,
And struck our oars against the salt-grey sea,
To reach the point which earlier we had marked
As that place where this strange tribe must be.
    We reached the land and found a high roofed cave
    Which to their flocks, at night, safe shelter gave.

118

A massive courtyard round the cave was made
Surrounded by tall pines and mighty oaks;
Each night a monstrous man slept in their shade;
He lived apart from all his kindred folk.
I bade most of my crew to stay behind,
But chose to take with me twelve of the best
To go inland that giant man to find,
I also took dark wine which Maro pressed:
Apollo's priest had given me that gift,
A potent drink and sweet, of vintage rare;
To find his cave, provisioned well, we left
And soon we found the entrance to his lair.
    The cave was empty with its lord far off,
    With sheep and goats, out pasturing his flock.

119

We went inside the cave and looked around
And gazed in wonder at the riches there;
Fat lambs and kids, in crowded pens we found
And crates of cheese and other tempting fare,
Which my companions urged that we should take,
Then go to our swift ships and leave with speed;
But curious: and fatal that mistake!
I bade them stay through arrogance and greed
To meet that man himself who lorded here;
In hope that he would give gifts from his store,
When he arrived we cowered back in fear
As with a mighty stone he sealed the door.
    We watched him as he milked his goats and sheep
    And lit his fire within that cavern deep.

120

Then seeing us, he asked us who we were
And how we'd journeyed 'cross the bounding waves.
I answered him, in terror and despair,
How we had come to find these awful caves.
We were men of Troy, Achaians all,
Who kneeled before him now as supplicants;
He said that we were fools this way to call,
None bowed before the god's omnipotence.
He asked about my ship but, craftily,
I told him that we few there had survived:
Poseidon had wrecked us on the sea
And on sharp rocks, nearby, the rest had died.
    His heart unmoved, the giant spoke no word,
    He sought to feed and see that none were spared.

121

He sprang and seized two of my comrades then
And dashed their brains out on the hard baked ground,
As puppies slaughtered by an owner when
No use or homes for all the brood is found.
He cut them limb from limb and crunched their bones,
Ate flesh and entrails leaving nothing spare.
We wailed and prayed to Zeus with piteous moans
At his cruel deeds, in helpless terror there.
The Cyclops drank fresh milk to end his feast
And then lay down within his cave to sleep;
Then with my sword I thought to slay that beast
Whilst deep in slumber lain amongst his sheep.
    But with his ending we too would have died
    Trapped by that door-stone, huge, to starve inside.

122

With wailing then, we waited for bright dawn,
And he awoke and morning's tasks renewed.
He lit the fire and milked his flocks in turn,
Then two from our small band he killed for food.
Now moving his great door-stone easily
He drove his flocks out from the cave to graze;
He then replaced the mighty stone and we
Were left in gloom, with hearts filled with malaise.
To pastures high the Cyclops drove his flocks
Whistling loudly as he went his way;
Whilst I planned evil, mid entombing rocks,
And thought out what to do at close of day.
    I cut a length off from the giant's club,
    Then sharpened to a point that olive wood.

123

With point then hardened in the blazing fire
I hid the stake within a pile of dung,
And then drew lots for four who would conspire
With me to chance our lives to right that wrong,
Which he had done to those of us he'd slain.
Thus when he returned at even-tide,
With his fat flocks, the cave he sealed again
And milked those goats and ewes close by his side,
Then placed them with their young. But then he seized
Two of my men, his night meal to provide.
I took him wine and said he might be pleased
To try a draught which he had never tried.
    He drained the cup and thought the taste so fine
    That three times more he asked for that dark wine.

124

The Cyclops asked my name and said: a gift
He'd give to me for this ambrosial drink.
Three times I saw the wine-full cup him lift
And drain, this helped his wits thus not to think.
I told him then—'Nobody' was my name!
He said that he would eat—'Nobody'— last.
That this would be the gift that I would gain;
Then reeling back to slumber he was cast
By that strong wine, which he had drunk with greed.
Then while he slept I seized the pointed stake
And laid it in the fire with urgent speed
And in red heat we left it there to bake.
    We seized it then and thrust it in his eye
    And ground it round; his sight thus to deny.

125

His single eyeball hissed and streamed black blood,
And he cried out aloud, in agony;
He wrenched the stake out flailing as he stood,
And we shrank back although he could not see.
He shouted to the Cyclopes who dwelled
In cave-homes near him on the windy heights;
They thronged around and asked him why he'd called,
In pain, thus stealing sleep from all their nights.
He told that tribe—'Nobody', was the cause!
And they replied that sickness thus must hold
Him there alone; advising, without pause,
That he should pray to have his woes consoled.
    On saying that they left and my heart smiled
    Within me, knowing they had been beguiled.

126

The Cyclops, groaning, groped towards the door
And took away the stone and sat on guard,
With arms outstretched there, waiting on the floor
For those who sought to go, if any dared.
In my mind I wove all sorts of schemes
To save us from sure death, which waited there,
His thick wooled rams at last gave me the means
For all to leave, with him still unaware.
I twisted bed withes underneath each fleece
Of chosen rams which then were flanked by two,
I hid a man beneath each middle beast;
They lay concealed away from touch or view.
    At last, I chose the largest of them all
    And clung beneath him till fair dawn would fall.

127

Then as day broke his fine rams hastened forth
To pasture, leaving ewes still in the pen;
The Cyclops felt their backs, but round their girth
He did not think to probe for my poor men.
Then last of all he stroked his largest beast
And asked him why he left now, last of all;
For he was first of all to leave and feast
On grass and drink from mountain streams which fall.
He said you surely sorrow for that eye
Which your kind master lost through this foul deed,
Done by that man who gave me wine to try,
It brought wit-dulling sleep on me with speed.
    'Nobody' is his name and sweet will be
    My dark revenge, should he now come near me.

128

On saying this he sent the ram to graze
Out from the cave and courtyard, to the fields,
I freed my comrades from each woolly maze
Beneath those sheep, well worn as safety's shields.
We drove those long-shanked beasts back to our ship
And there were welcomed by the waiting crew,
Then saw the sorrowed pangs of mourning grip
Each man when tidings of those dead he knew.
Yet weeping I forbade and told them load
With speed those fine fleeced sheep, and then we sailed,
This done they took their bench seats all and rowed;
Against the grey seas, biting, long blades flailed
    To carry us a shouts length from the beach,
    Safe, I thought, beyond the Cyclops' reach.

129

I turned to bate him then with mocking jibe
And said his evil deeds had been repaid;
Then angered by my sharp barbed diatribe
He broke a mountain peak—I watched dismayed
As out to sea he flung it just beyond
Our ship, which rose and drove back on the surge;
I seized a spar to stop us reaching land,
For if beached, where shore and sea converge,
The giant there our vessel he might clasp.
I urged my comrades: "row with urgent haste"
To save the ship from Polyphemus' grasp,
They drove us swift across the salty waste
    Till twice as far from land as previously,
    We stayed, I thought to rest there now, safely.

130

I turned once more to goad that savage man,
Though all my comrades begged me to refrain;
But anger ruled my heart and I began
And told him who I was with cold disdain —
From Ithaca I came: Laertes' son!
The Cyclops groaned, replying with the word
Of woe—because the prophecy had come,
From Telemus their seer it had been heard.
He said Odysseus would take my sight,
And I looked for a strong and handsome man,
Not some weakling plotting in the night,
To blind me with his sly and dreadful plan.
 He asked me then to row back to the beach
 And rich gifts would he give, when in his reach.

131

He said to the great sea god he was son,
And he would ask him for our quick return.
From him wished healing to his eye might come
And swift conveyance from this isle would earn.
I said if able I would take his soul
And send him down to Hades far below:
Poseidon then could never make him whole,
He'd stay forever blind and wracked with woe.
He prayed then to the great god of the sea
That his tormentor never should reach home,
Or if he did his final destiny
Would take him back without his men, alone:
 There to find his household full of strife,
 With faithless knaves dishonouring his wife.

132

The prayer was heard, but in his rage and pain
The Cyclops lifted up a mighty peak
And threw it far across the foaming main,
Attempting thus the fleeing ship to reach.
It landed close, and drove us to that isle
Where all the other ships lay on the sands;
We drove the flocks out pausing there a while
To share those beasts amongst each swift ship's hands.
An extra ram they gave to me alone
So I to Zeus might make a sacrifice,
In hope to win his favour and atone
For any wrong, but this did not suffice.
    We feasted, then took rest till dawn arose
    And then embarked weighed down by thoughts morose.

Book 10

133

Aoleus' dreaming island we found next,
Dear to the gods that keeper of the winds;
A wall of bronze that floating land protects
And mighty cliffs its noble halls defends.
Six daughters and six sons as man and wife
Live there feasted by his goodly cheer;
We spent a month there telling of that strife
We'd found at Troy and that which drove us here.
And when I asked him if I might depart
He gave me aid beyond necessity,
An ox skin then he filled by his great art
With all the blustering winds which rouse the sea.
    For Zeus the son of Cronos gave him sway
    To rouse or quiet storm winds as he may.

134

Aoleus bound his winds within my ship,
Tight in their ox skin, with a silver cord,
So not a breath could from the leather slip
To change our course or drive huge waves on board.
He sent the West Wind forth to bear us home,
We sailed nine days and nights till almost there,
Then on the tenth across the wave tossed foam
We saw our home fires on that island fair.
But then the gods brought down on me sweet sleep,
For weariness, caused by unceasing toil,
Swept over me that blissful slumber deep,
Which is night's gift which soothes long days turmoil.
    But whilst I slept that demon: envy, came;
    My comrades asked, what did the skin contain?

135

They thought I'd saved some treasure for myself,
And opened up the oxhide bag to see—
The winds safe bound there were its only wealth
And they rushed out as gales, tempestuously;
To sweep those miscreants, weeping, out to sea.
Then I awoke and pondered in my heart
Should I endure with them that destiny
Or jump there from the ship, and life depart!
But I endured in silence and remained,
Wrapped in my cloak against the evil blast
Till we once more Aoleus' isle regained—
By mocking fate upon its shoreline cast.
    They went inland and drew fresh water, sweet,
    Then by the ships we all sat down to eat.

136

With herald and one comrade then I went
Back to the palace of Aoleus;
Amazed he asked what demon foul had sent
Us there, when we'd embarked with Zephyrus
To fill our sails, till we came home once more.
I told him how my comrades ruined me
And asked for help, but he said nevermore!
He told me to be gone for he could see
That I was hated by the gods on high;
Thus I left him, groaning mightily,
And we strove on with no breeze in the sky;
For seven long days we rowed across the sea.
    We came then to the Laestrogonian lands
    And found a harbour where its sheer cliff stands.

137

There, nights are short and days run endlessly;
Thus if a man could manage without sleep
And take two herds, he'd earn a double fee,
With cattle marshalled first and then white sheep.
Outside that port I moored my ship, alone,
Whilst all the others anchored theirs inside;
I then climbed high upon a rugged stone,
From there I looked around me far and wide,
I saw no men or oxen, only smoke,
Which rose and told of habitation there;
I chose three men to go and seek its folk,
They set off down a road worn smooth and bare
    By wagons which brought wood down from the hills
    To feed red fires, and ward of winter's ills.

138

They met the daughter of Antiphates
Who'd come down to Artacia, a spring,
Whose pure bright water flows with endless ease
To feed the needs of commoner and king.
They asked her who was ruler of that place:
And she showed them her father's high roofed hall.
They went within and there came face to face
With his wife, a giantess so tall
That my men who saw her were aghast,
And seeing this she called Antiphates
Who seized one there to make him his repast;
The others fled down to the shore-side quays.
    The king raised up a cry throughout their town
    And Laestrogonians all came thronging down.

139

From those cliffs they pelted us with rocks,
And from the crews then rose a dreadful din
As seamen died within those awful docks
Crushed then speared from ships left there in ruin.
I cut the cables of my vessel then,
For we alone were placed where we could flee,
Thus to the oars I, urgent, set my men
To row and seek the safety of the sea.
From there we sailed though grieving in our hearts,
For only our sleek vessel now remained,
Until we reached that Isle of magic arts
Called Aeaea, thereon a fair witch reigned
    Called Circe, who from Helios was sprung
    And from the goddess Perse's womb was won.

140

In doleful sorrow there we disembarked
And spent two days in feasting comrades lost;
When Dawn rose on the third day from her bed
With that grief dimmed, I felt the seeker's lust
And took my sword and trusty spear to go
Up to those rugged heights, to survey all.
Down in the woods and thickets spread below
I saw smoke rising from fair Circe's hall;
I pondered in my mind if I should go
To find which hand had caused that plume to rise,
But thought it best to first go back below
And feed my men before that enterprise.
    Then climbing down I came across a stag
    Descending there, to drink from its high crag.

141

I struck the high horned beast with my bronze spear,
His noble spirit fled with a last moan,
I wove a rope from twigs of osier,
To bind its feet and bear its weight alone.
Across my back then, leaning on my lance,
I stumbled down and made my comrades glad,
That such a feast had come our way by chance
To lift despair and end those weeks so bad.
We dined all day and slept then, well content,
But at the dawn I called my men and said
That to explore the isle was my intent,
But they our giant foes remembered
　　And though they feared I formed them in two bands,
　　One to stay and one to search those lands.

142

Eurylochus, then leading twenty two,
Set off into the dark foreboding wood,
Though concerned, a house soon came in view
Around which wolves and mountain lions stood.
These beasts had Circe with her drugs bewitched,
And they came wagging tails like friendly hounds;
They stood within her gate, in fear, and watched
And heard her sing and marvelled at those sounds.
With sweetest voice she sang and worked her loom
And wove a web of splendour and great size;
Polites cried out loud into her room,
This caused the witch, up from her work, to rise
　　And open her great doors and take them in
　　With welcome smile, their confidence to win.

143

Eurylochus, alone, refrained to dine
For he suspected this could be a snare;
He watched as she brought seats and Pramian wine
And drug laced food to keep them in her lair.
Of honey, sweet, and cheese they all partook
And that drink which caused them to forget,
Then with her wand at once those fools she struck
And trapped them spell bound, pig-like, in her debt,
In pens, and flung them nuts and mast to eat;
Euryloychus, who saw this, swift returned
To tell us all of Circe's foul deceit
And how his men to swine-like forms were turned.
　　I armed myself with sword and mighty bow
　　Preparing to the sorceress to go.

144

Eurylochus, in terror, asked to stay,
But I was bound by honour to return,
Back to those sacred glades where Circe lay
In wait for those whom her drugged charms would earn.
On leaving, Hermes, of the golden wand,
Met me in the likeness of a youth,
And asked me if to free my men I planned,
He warned me that without his aid, in truth,
That I would also fall beneath her spell;
To keep me safe he picked a guardian herb
Called Moly, milky flowered, which gods knew well,
Whose qualities foul witchcraft's evils curb.
　　Whilst Hermes back to high Olympus went
　　I neared the witch-lair, wary, ill-content.

145

The god had told me all which must be done
When Circe struck me with her magic wand,
That I must draw my sword and rush upon
The sorceress, with threatening blade in hand.
I stood and called, the goddess heard my shout
And opened her bright doors and showed me in,
And sat me down then poured her potion out
Into a golden cup; to bring me ruin.
I drank the draught—she struck me with her wand
And bade me go to lie down in my sty;
Amazing her, ignoring her command,
I drew the sword which lay beside my side.
    I rushed at her; she thought that death was near
    And cried aloud and clasped my knees in fear.

146

With wailing words she asked me whence I came
For no man ever had withstood her charm,
Hermes had said: "one day a man of fame
Odysseus may call, and do her harm."
She begged me thus to lie with her in bed;
Comingling our love in search of trust.
"Why should I be gentle now", I said,
"And in your chamber pleasure you in lust,
For you have turned my comrades into swine!
First you must swear an oath to now abstain
From mischief made by sorcery divine,
Or cause me hurt, or bring me further pain."
    She swore as I had asked then quickly led,
    Me not unwilling to her fabled bed.

147

Her handmaids meanwhile busied in her halls,
They were children of sweet springs and groves
And sacred streams, whose blessed water falls
Down to the sea through cliffs and secret coves.
One threw purple rugs upon each chair
And spread beneath them all a linen shawl;
Another brought out golden dining ware
To set on silver tables in her hall.
A third mixed honeyed wine, the sweetest kind,
A fourth boiled water in a bronze cauldron
To bath me, and my weariness unbind,
Anointing me with oil when that was done.
    She dressed me in a cloak and tunic fine,
    Then brought me down into her hall to dine.

148

They sat me down, with footstool for my feet,
With water poured into a silver dish,
To wash in when with food I was replete,
For more was laid out there than I could wish.
I did not put my hands out to the food
And Circe noticed I was bound by grief,
With anxious words she asked what caused this mood
Of sorrow and how she might bring relief.
I said my comrade's bondage made me sad:
Thus Circe went at once to set them free;
Removing pig like features which they had,
Restoring them to youth which all could see.
    On their release they sobbed and clutched my hands
    At their ordeal within those witch ruled lands.

149

The sorceress drew near to me and said:
"Go now to draw your ship up on the land
And in the caves your goods and tackle spread,
Then please return, with your good sailor band."
My heart consented to her sweet request,
And all were keen to come back to her halls
To eat and drink, except for one: the best,
Eurylochus, who said what might befall:
We might be turned once more to wolves or swine;
My anger nearly brought out my sharp blade
But comrade's pleas just checked my ire in time,
Then all went with me, no-one disobeyed.
     Arriving then amongst their ship mates midst
     They wept in greeting, thinking they were lost.

150

The goddess ordered—end your sad lament,
And told us that she knew well all our woes,
Inviting us to eat till well content,
We feasted a full year, safe from our foes.
The seasons turned and at those sweet months end
My trusty comrades spoke once more of home;
When sunset came I begged Circe to send
Us once more on our way, grey seas to roam.
She granted our release yet said I must,
At first, to dreaded Hades go to find
The ghost of blind Tiresias to ask
The Theban of the those visions in his mind.
     For he alone in death had reason still
     Granted by Persephone's great will.

151

In dread I wept, with no desire for life,
But when that ended asked her for a guide,
She said our way was clear and free from strife
For on the North-wind's breath our ship would ride,
Across deep Oceanus to a grove
Sacred to Death's queen: Persephone.
There willows wept and poplars reached above,
In mourning, for all those who cease to be.
There, into Acheron flows Phlegethon,
Cocytus too, a branch of dreadful Styx;
Where these two meet Hell's entrance might be won
If with red wine you might ram's dark blood mix.
    The seer must come to you to point your way
    To bring you home at last without delay.

152

With Dawn descended from her golden throne
She dressed me, knowing this must be farewell.
Then donned a long white robe with golden zone
And round her face the veil of sadness fell.
Now I went through her halls and roused my men
To tell them Circe said that we could go;
I could not lead them safely, even then,
For Elphenor the youngest brought sorrow;
For sleeping on the roof, heavy with wine,
He sprang from sleep, unwarily, and fell
And broke his neck, cursed by the fates malign
To go to Hades where all lost shades dwell.
    Circe left a ram and a black ewe
    Beside our ship, to aid what I must do.

Book 11

153

We drew the black ship down onto the sea
And loaded all the sheep and gear aboard,
A fair wind filled our sails, thus easily
We slipped across the waves, past lands abhorred,
Locked forever in perpetual night;
There Cimmerians never see the sun.
At last our destination came in sight
And up the beach our sturdy ship was run.
With sacrificial beast held by my men
I drew my sword and dug a cubit, square,
Round the pit I poured libation then
With milk and wine, and honey to prepare
    It for white barley scattered to entreat
    The dead from Hades, summoned here to meet.

154

I vowed on reaching Ithaca again
My finest heifer I would sacrifice,
And place the richest gifts from my domain
Upon the altar, those shades to entice.
I promised I would sacrifice a ram,
All black, to blind Tiresias alone.
I slew the sheep and down the black blood ran
Into the pit to call the dead ones home.
They gathered from the depths of Erebus,
All kinds of ghosts, from youths to new wed brides;
Toil worn old men and pink skinned virgins plus
Great blood stained soldiers, crowding on all sides.
    I told my men to burn the sheep and pray,
    Whilst I with sword blade kept those shades at bay.

155

Pale fear had seized me hearing their dread cry,
And first to come was new dead Elphenor,
Who in Circe's house was last to die;
He dwelt amongst the shades now, evermore.
In our haste we'd left him in her hall
Without the proper rites or burial,
I promised, going home, that we would call
And burn him with all fitting ritual,
Then pile his ashes near the swelling sea
And fix an oar, in memory, in his mound.
I vowed such would become his destiny,
While still I held my sword above the ground
    Above the blood, forbidding all to drink
    Until the seer came forth to that pit's brink.

156

Next my mother Anticles came near,
Her life had ended while I fought at Troy;
Though pity filled my heart I knew the seer
Must be the first the blood-draught to enjoy.
Then his ghost arose, gold staff in hand,
He knew me asking why I had come there;
I drew back from the pit at his command,
Then sheathed my sword so he could drink his share
Of that dark blood and bring his prophecy.
He drank and told me how I might return
Despite the anger of the god-of-sea;
My longed for island home I still could earn.
    He warned me at Thrinacea to leave
    The cattle, safe unharmed, or I would grieve.

157

For these belong to Helios who sees
All things and thus his curse will bring down ill,
On those who disobey my stern decrees,
Which, if obeyed, will all your dreams fulfil.
But if you choose the sun god's beasts to slay
I see the ruin of your ship and crew;
But even so, back to your isle one day
You will return, to find those knaves who woo
Your lady wife and waste your livelihood;
And you will have revenge upon them all.
He told me then to take an oar of wood
And go inland, where seabirds never call,
    Till far from any coast I met a man
    Who would think that oar a threshing fan.

158

He told me, there in earth to fix that blade,
And to Poseidon make great offerings,
With ram and bull and boar on altar laid,
Then homeward go to end my journeying.
Then when safe to offer hecatombs
To those immortals holding heaven's realms;
Thus gentle death will take you when it comes,
In sleek old age when darkness overwhelms.
I asked the seer about my mother's shade
And how she yet may recognise her son—
He said: "whoever drinks the blood is made
Once more to know this world where life is run;
    They must speak true whom you permit to drink,
    Those you refuse will back to Hades sink."

159

Whilst the seer descended back below
My mother rose and drank, and knew me then;
With mournful wailing words she asked me how
I'd come to Hades from the world of men.
I told her of my journeying and pain
And asked how into this domain she'd come
And sought to know of those who yet remain
In Ithaca: my father, wife and son.
She said my wife held firm, yet un-possessed,
And my stout son still lorded my estates,
My father, though in old age, she confessed,
In sorrow, for your coming home still waits.
 She said that all her longing and despair
 For my return, brought death, which bore her there.

160

I longed to take her to me to console,
And three times sprang towards her ghost and tried;
Yet three times her eluding shadow stole
Out of my grasp and those attempts denied.
I asked her if she was a phantom sent
By dread Persephone to taunt my mind;
I wished to hold her there in last lament
And through that weeping some last comfort find.
My mother answered this must be the way
When blazing fire destroys our last remains,
That spirit only, like a dream, holds sway
Within those realms which end all mortal pains.
 We talked a while and other women came,
 Wives and daughters of past chiefs of fame.

161

I let them drink the dark blood one by one,
Then each declared her birth and who she'd been
The first was high born Tyro who was won
By Poseidon, though longing to be queen
Of that river fairest of them all;
The crafty sea-god took his flowing form
And lay with her hid by those waves which fall
Where rivers end, and breaking seas are born.
Pelius and Neleus she bore
Who ruled Iolocus and sandy isle
Of Pylos, then had mortal children more
To Cretheus, in happy domicile.
    I saw Antiope who slept with Zeus
    And bore Amphision and Zetheus.

162

After her I saw fair Alcmene,
Who, loved by Zeus gave birth to Heracles
And Megara, high Creon's daughter she,
And there the mother of Oedipodes.
Epicaste: wed to her own son!
Who hung herself when finding out the truth.
That monstrous deed in ignorance was done,
Yet brought down countless woes on that sad youth.
I then met Chloris who great Nestor bore,
And Pero who was sought out by all men,
Given as wife though when high Nileus saw
The beasts of Iphicles brought to him then
    By Melanpus, who won her by that feat,
    Which many months had taken to complete.

163

And Leda then, wife to Tyndareus
Who bore him twins: Castor, Polydeuces;
In Hades now they still receive from Zeus:
Life, which on alternate days each frees.
Iphimedeia came, who said she'd lain
With great Poseidon, bearing him two sons:
Otus and Ephiphaltes who sought fame
By threats against the great Olympians.
Though giants, they were slain before their time
By Leto's son Apollo, in their youth.
Others rose, the godlike and malign,
To tell of them would take all night in truth.
    I told them I was weary and confessed
    I must now there, or in my swift ship rest.

164

They all fell silent, spellbound at my words;
The queen Arête then was first to speak
And said that I must sleep amongst their lords,
Within her hall wrapped round by slumber deep.
Alcinous then said, till break of day,
I should remain there as their honoured guest,
Then bearing gifts I, swift, should make my way
But now should hold back from my well earned rest,
And go on with this tale of those from Troy.
I told them then how Agamemnon came
To drink the blood, to speak, bereft of joy,
Of how foul murder ended his long reign.
    Which Clytemnestra planned, though still his wife;
    By foul Aegisthus he was robbed of life.

165

While feasting were himself and comrades slain,
With fair Cassandra, Priam's daughter too;
Her piteous cries still here with me remain,
Dark Clytemnestra that poor maiden slew.
The bitch then turned away and did not choose
To close my eyes as down to death I went;
With hatred shown thus by that foul abuse
With curses into Hades I was sent.
I told him others of his noble line
Were punished or condemned by women's guile;
First Helen's beauty brought down wrath divine;
Caused many deaths, and then my long exile.
 He gave advice—to always be severe
 To women, even those which you hold dear!

166

He asked me if Orestes still survived;
But as a mortal man I could not know
What fate he'd met, or how the gods connived
To give him greatness or to bring him low.
While there we stood exchanging mourning words
The ghost of great Achilles rose to speak,
He asked me why I'd summoned those dead lords
From Hades depths, their sorrowed words to seek.
I said I'd sought Tiresias through need
Of knowledge how to reach my rugged home;
I told that greatest hero not to grieve
That he among the dead was bound to roam.
 For he with the immortal gods was held,
 In honour, for his deeds, unparalleled.

167

He said that he would rather be alive
And be the basest hireling of some lord,
Or landless, barely able to survive,
Than rule the dead, within those realms abhorred.
He asked me if his father: Peleus,
Was honoured still among the Myrmidons;
I only knew of Neoptolemus:
His son, and all the victories he'd won
Against the Trojans on their dusty plain;
I knew that from those wars he'd left unscathed,
With booty gained and with immortal fame
For deeds still sung of and great dangers braved.
    Then with great strides across the Asphodel
    Achilles went, to where long shadows dwell.

168

All the others asked me then of home,
And all those longed for loved ones left behind
Apart from Aias, who stood off alone,
For angry pride still filled his noble mind,
That in the funeral games he'd failed and lost
Achilles' armour which he greatly prized;
Defeated by myself to his great cost,
Shamed by the gods he thought and in men's eyes.
Though past the Lethe he could not forget
That flawless son of mighty Telamon,
I told him of the sorrow and regret
Of all the Greeks for their great warrior son.
    Though I spoke he answered not a word,
    But turned away with all my pleas unheard.

169

I then saw Minos in that Stygian gloom,
Sat with a golden sceptre in his hand
In judgement over all those spectres whom
Were bound by death, each under his command.
I then saw great Orion herding still
Those beasts that he had slain mid lonely hills,
And Tityus lying stretched where vultures shrill
Still tear his liver as the god-king wills,
For raping Leto, his own consort dear;
And Tantalus I saw, in torment great,
With water rising round him cool and clear
But when he stooped to drink, such was his fate,
 The water vanished leaving dry black earth
 And when he reached for fruit he found their dearth.

170

I then saw Sisyphus in bitter pain,
Forever bound to roll a mighty stone,
Up a hill, but when its high peak came
That mass was fated then to roll back down.
After him great Heracles arose
In phantom form, still with the gods he feasts;
And there as wife the goddess Hebe chose,
And in those realms his spirit never sleeps
But roams with readied bow, and terror brings
Amid the shades who shriek as birds in flight;
Around his breast a golden baldric hangs
Embossed with deeds and creatures of the night
 Wild eyed beasts and battles, murders dark;
 All those slayings which his war crafts mark.

171

He knew me when he saw me there and spoke,
Asking me what evil lot I bore,
Or if I laboured under a cruel yoke,
Like him, with tasks decreed by some god's law.
Once in the past he went to Hades' gates
And stole the hound which guards the way below,
The hardest of those labours which the Fates
On him, in life, were able to bestow.
He turned and left and I became afraid
Lest from those depths the Gorgon's head should rise,
Thus back down to the ship my way I made,
And we embarked beneath those sullen skies.
        Then Oceanus bore us from that shore
        With aid of fair set winds and skilful oar.

Book 12

172

Our ship came through the waves to Circe's isle
And when Dawn rose we brought down Elphenor,
And burned his corpse then heaped into a pile
His armour as he'd asked, and placed an oar
Upon the mound to mark the place he lay.
Then with her maids the goddess Circe came
And laid out meats and bread in fine array,
And sparkling wine, red, rich with summer's flame.
She spoke amongst us saying: "stubborn men!
Who now must meet death twice in Hades' halls;
Come! Eat and drink for when day comes again
You must embark to where your home isle calls.
　　Thus I will show the route which you must take
　　And tell you of those dangers which still wait."

173

At sunset, Circe took me by the hand
And led me off, and lay with me and asked,
What strange things we had found in that far land
Which we had come to in those weeks just past.
I told her all, then regal Circe spoke
About those dangers which we still must find,
And told me of those wiles I must invoke
To win our way and leave her far behind.
I heard then of the sirens, who by guile
Entrap poor souls with sweetness of their song;
They sit where heaps of rotting men defile
The air, and deaths vile stench hangs overlong.
　　She ordered: "stop the ears of all your men
　　With wax, so they might pass in safety then!

174

If I willed to listen to those two
I must command my comrades: tie me fast!
With ropes so tight that I could not undo
Those cords which bound me to our ships tall mast,
And if I should demand that I be freed
Then they should tie me tighter than before;
The siren's song's enchantment brings such need
To stay with them in death upon their shore."
She told me then about the Plactae crags,
Against which roar great Amphitrite's waves;
"No bird may pass, not even timorous doves,
Some are snatched and go to watery graves.
    Of ships which came there none have passed but one:
    Only Jason's, Hera smiled upon.

175

And on the other side rise cliffs, smooth worn,
Their peaks are always shrouded in dark mists;
High up some see a dim lit cave mouth yawn,
Within its maw the monstrous Scylla sits.
The creature has twelve legs and squats within,
While six long necks extend above the sea
Each head has teeth—three rows as black as sin;
Each takes a man from passing ships as fee.
The other cliff is lower, yet beneath
Its walls Charybdis sucks black water down;
Three times a day she draws in whirling breath
And three times from her gut the stream is blown.
    Avoid those hours when rushing waters fall
    For in those torrents death must come to all."

176

Circe said: "pass close to Scylla's cave,
Your loss will then be six men and not all."
I asked if force of arms might these souls save;
The goddess said: "with speed, just six must fall.
Against this dread immortal none could fight,
Call upon her mother Crataeis
To hold her back, then row with all your might
And save most of your crew from death's Abyss.
Then Thrinacea's Island you will find,
Where sheep and oxen of the sun god feed,
Seven flocks of each, but not the mortal kind
They cannot die, thus do not need to breed.
    Two daughter's of Hyperion—shepherds there,
    Their mother Neaera, of beauty rare.

177

Phaethusa and Lampetis are their names:
Fair nymphs who guard their father's herds and flocks;
Whoever harms them death and ruin gains,
You must thus take a warning from my words."
Then Circe left, departing with bright Dawn
And I roused up my comrades to embark.
We loosed the cables keen to be sea-born
Then took our oars and launched our speedy barque.
A fair wind filled our sail, which Circe sent,
With helmsman steering all the crew sat down,
And I spoke of our peril as we went
Towards the Siren's island, I alone
    Must be allowed to hear them, though tied well,
    As we sailed past those meadows where they dwell.

178

I kneaded wax to stop my comrade's ears
And they then bound me, upright, to the mast.
They all sat down and struck hard with their oars
The deep grey sea to drive our swift ship past
That deadly Island, where the sirens sang
To me in praise, with beauty in each voice.
Seductive pleas above the wave tops rang;
I begged then for release, with little choice
Eurylochus, Perimedes, arose
And bound me tighter, till those voices ceased.
Thus freed at last from sweet enchantments throes
My ears were cleansed, and then I was released.
    One danger past, another came in sight,
    With booming sounds ahead the crew took fright.

179

But I went through the ship to cheer my men
Reminding them of evils overcome,
And our escape from Cyclops' evil pen
And how to safety from his ire we'd run.
I told them all to keep their seats and beat
The deep surf of the sea with their stout oars,
So with the help of Zeus we could defeat
That peril, if we speeded without pause.
Yet in the heat of danger I forgot
The hard command of Circe—not to arm!
I donned my armour then my long spears sought
To stand and keep my comrades free from harm.
    I kept the secret though of Scylla's curse
    As through the straits we ran, on our traverse.

180

Charybdis sucked the sea into his bowels
Then belched it forth—those waters seemed to boil,
As seething spray burst forth from her great jowls,
Foul terror bound my men in its strong coil
As they stared down into her awful maw.
Then from above us Scylla sought out six
And took them, writhing, gripped in each great jaw.
They called my name though doomed to cross the Styx,
For then the monster drew them to her cave
And at its entrance each man shrieked and cried;
While she devoured them each implored my aid
But I could rescue none and thus all died.
    Of all things which I bore on my journey
    The worst was hearing them cry, piteously.

181

We left those straits and came unto the isle
Of Helios Hyperion where stood
His many flocks, remembering the while:
Tiresias; who warned me that no good
Would come if we set foot upon his shore;
And Circe, who advised that we should shun
Those pastures or find dangers held in store;
I urged my comrades, pass the isles and run
And row and seek the safety of the sea,
But they were worn by toil and lack of sleep
Desiring rest within some sheltered lea—
I made them swear an oath which they must keep:
    They must not touch the sun gods sacred herds!
    They all agreed they would—with hollow words.

182

I urged them to partake of Circe's grain,
But then some god conspired to seal our fate,
And for a full month only south winds came;
Thus all the stores we'd brought my comrades ate.
Thus they grew hungry and sought fish and game,
And I went inland so that I might pray,
But all the gods were deaf and no winds came
To fill our sails and take us on our way.
The Olympians though shed sleep upon my eyes
And then Eurylochus spoke evil words:
That from the Sun god's herds they sacrifice
Upon the altar with their sharp edged swords.
    He told them for this deed they might atone
    With temples built for Helios back home.

183

But when that deed was done sweet slumber fled
And I went down to where our ship was beached.
The smell of roasting filled my heart with dread,
I groaned aloud and all the gods beseeched,
For they had brought down ruin on my men
By lulling me, off guard, with gentle sleep.
To Helios came swift Lampetis then
To tell him of his slaughtered kine and sheep.
He asked great Zeus to bring down vengeance, swift,
And let my men, with awful death, atone
For that deed and his dark anger lift.
If not paid back he may bright heaven disown
    And go to Hades, by black anger led,
    And in that kingdom shine among the dead.

184

With speed Zeus answered, asking him to stay,
To shed his light on gods and mortals too;
For he with thunderbolts would make them pay,
Those whom the sun god's straight horned cattle, slew.
I sought my men, upbraiding each in turn,
But what was done could never be reversed;
Then portents came which said that deed would earn
A payment fit for those the gods had cursed.
We saw hides crawl and heard meat slaughtered, raw:
Bellow! Then came lowing cattle sounds
To warn them they had broken sacred law,
Thus soon would follow vengeance's wild hounds.
    In gloom we feasted there for six long days,
    Storm bound on that Island of malaise.

185

The seventh day came, at last the harsh wind ceased,
And thus we went aboard and set our sail;
No land appeared, yet lowering cloud increased
And dark waves rose blown by a shrieking gale.
The forestays snapped and sternwards dropped the mast
And crushed the steer-mans skull and down he fell;
Upon the ship Zeus hurled his mighty blast,
And swept my crew into that heaving swell.
Like sea crows they were swept about the ship
Yet Zeus ensured they never would return;
I paced the deck and heard the side planks rip
Then watched the mast snap off and fall astern.
    But with an oxhide backstay, keel and mast,
    I lashed as one and rode the stormy blast.

186

But then the winds reversed and bore me back
Towards Charybdis, filling me with dread!
For down into her maw she sucked my craft,
Whilst I clung to a fig tree, overhead.
I waited till she spewed my poor craft out,
Then when it came I dropped into the swell
And climbed aboard, then rowed yet kept lookout
For Scylla, keeping low and all was well.
For Zeus ensured out of her sight I passed
Through those narrow straits to open sea;
For nine days then I drifted till at last
I came to rest in Ogyis' sheltered lea.
 There the fair haired nymph Calypso dwells,
 As you well know; a fool that tale retells.

Book 13

187

All were spellbound, silent, in those halls
Until Alcinous made his reply,
"He said that now your final journey calls,
With many gifts we soon must say goodbye."
When rosy fingered dawn rose in the east
They hastened to the ship to stow below
Its benches, all their bounty, then a feast
Was ordered by the king, but keen to go
Odysseus fretted through the sacrifice
And feasting, while the minstrel sang and played;
Impatient that this farewell would suffice
To mark departure overlong delayed.
    He asked the king, towards the end of day:
    "With last libations, send me on my way."

188

The guest then asked the gods to bless his host
And said: "at home he hoped all things were well."
They praised his words and with one final toast
All poured libations, fair winds to compel.
Prontonous served out the honeyed wine;
Odysseus rose and placed within the hands
Of Arête, his cup, with words divine:
He asked that joy should always fill her lands.
Then with a herald leading him he left
And passed down to the ship upon the shore;
A slave girl carried down the gift filled chest,
Two others drink and food and clothing bore.
    The young lords laid out bedding for their guest,
    So whilst they rowed Odysseus might rest.

189

They loosed the hawser from the huge pierced stone
Then sat to row, and struck the deep blue brine
With oar blades, as they did so he alone
Fell into death like sleep while they sped home.
The ship leapt high as drawn by stallions strong
Who spring together, urged on by the whip;
The wake foamed, gleaming, as she sped along;
No swift winged hawk could keep pace with that ship
Which bore a man wise as the gods are wise,
Who'd suffered many griefs on land and sea;
Then when the morning star rose in the skies
Landfall came, to end his long journey.
 At Ithaca at last, they came to land,
 And beached their ship high up upon the strand.

190

In Phorcys' harbour—old man of the sea—
They came to rest between two great headlands.
Above it grows a long leaved olive tree
And near that spot a shaded cavern stands,
Sacred to the Naiads, who inside
On long stone looms their webs of purple weave.
There the bees in jars their honey hide,
And two unfailing springs the rock floor cleave.
A door which men may use stands to the north
And one for gods, alone the south wind sees.
Below this sacred place the ship made berth,
Odysseus then they lifted up with ease
 And left him sleeping on the lonely sand,
 With all his gear stowed, hidden, near at hand.

191

Poseidon spoke in anger then to Zeus
Of how Odysseus gained such rewards,
He told him he was minded to reduce
That ship to flotsam, striking keel and yards;
To warn all the Phaeacians to desist
And cease from giving aid to mortal men,
Then hide their city in concealing mist,
Behind a cliff-face, huge, encircling them.
Zeus then answered, saying it seemed best
In his view to turn the ship to stone!
Near Scheris then he smote it with his fist
And left that rock as warning near their home.
    Those who saw that ship of stone appear
    Where a craft had been were seized by fear.

192

Alcinous spoke to that company,
Recalling ancient oracles which told:
How through Poseidon's anger they would see,
Him, round their city, misty mountains fold
And cause one of their ships to turn to stone
For giving swift conveyance to a man.
He said: "now we must act to save our home
By giving sacrifice from all our clan."
Then, while twelve choicest bulls were sacrificed
Odysseus woke, a stranger in his land!
He wondered where he was for mist disguised
Familiar ways—spread by Athene's hand.
    She wished to keep him hidden till he knew
    Who had wronged his name, and what to do!

193

Springing to his feet Odysseus groaned
And struck his mighty thighs, then asked aloud
What was this place he now, on waking, found!
He felt despair's dark thoughts around him crowd.
He thought the swift Phaeacians broke their word,
To leave him on some wild and fearsome isle.
He checked his treasure, making sure that hoard
Had all been left with him in his exile.
Of all those riches promised he missed none,
But nothing cheered him, on the shore he mourned
For his native land with all hope gone
For him to reach that place for which he yearned.
  But then Athene, as a youth, grew near
  And at that sight his heart filled with good cheer.

194

She stood there as a shepherd with a spear,
And round her shoulders wore a well wrought cloak;
Odysseus spoke to her as she drew near,
Enquiring of this island and its folk.
He asked her help to save those goods he'd brought,
Then flashing eyed Athene swift replied,
To say this was the island he'd long sought:
That 'Ithaca', to him so long denied.
Then, though the much enduring lord was glad,
With cunning words he sought to conceal all,
And spun a yarn of how Phoenicians had
Left him as guardian of their haul.
  The goddess smiled and stroked him with her hand,
  Then changed her form so he would understand.

195

Thus, like a woman beautiful and tall
She stood before him now, a goddess fair,
And told him that great dangers still must fall
Upon his head, which he must stoutly bear.
Then he, of many cunning wiles, replied:
That through many trials he'd asked her aid
To ward off sorrow, but had been denied
All help till on Phaeacian shores he'd laid.
He doubted yet that he had come safe home
And asked if this was truly his own isle?
She then described the paths he used to roam
On Ithaca, before his long exile.
    She cleared the mists so he could look upon
    His native land, and tree clothed Neriton.

196

Then Odysseus kissed the fertile earth
And prayed to all the nymphs with outstretched hands,
That waiting still his son of noble birth
Should live with him and grow to rule his lands.
Athene then assured him all was well
And said: "that they must now his treasure hide
Deep in that cave, where all the Naiads dwell
And then how to regain his lands: decide."
She told him how Penelope still mourned,
Whilst suitors wooed with gifts to take his place,
And how they all with mocking offers scorned
Her hope of his return, which gave solace.
    He knew then if he went to his halls straight
    That he would share great Agamemnon's fate.

197

The two sat near the sacred olive tree,
To scheme; devising death for suitors all.
Odysseus said at first he wished that she
Would stand beside him, then those knaves would fall.
She said she would be with him in his task,
But first must fast disguise his form to men:
With matted hair and shrivelled skin as mask,
In rags, he could in safety talk with them.
She said that she would dim his shining eyes
And make him look unseemly before all;
She told him then to go in that disguise
And on his faithful swineherd, firstly, call.
    She told him: "wait by Arethusa's spring
    Whilst I from Sparta your proud son, fast, bring.

198

Near here your herdsman sits, by Corax' rock,
His swine gorge acorns to their hearts content;
There, wait beside him by his fat livestock,
And talk with him of how his days are spent.
Odysseus asked the goddess of his son,
And wondered if he suffered on the seas.
She told him of the good report he'd won,
He now with Menelaus took his ease.
Then Athene touched him with her wand
Transforming him to seem an aged serf,
With ragged cloak and stout staff in his hand
And much holed pouch, and garments grained with dirt.
    With him disguised she left to fetch his son
    Journeying to far Lacedaemon.

Book 14

199

Odysseus made his way by the rough trail
Up from the harbour to the woodlands, where:
Set on high within that leafy vale
He found the swineherd, seated, resting there
Before his house, built with a splendid view,
Surrounded by a thorn topped court which penned
Great herds of swine, while he kept overview
Of savage dogs, which all his gear defend.
The herdsman cut out sandals from oxhide
Whilst round about him, guarding droves of swine
The fierce hounds wandered round his courtyard wide.
Now when they sensed him come, with growls malign,
    They rushed upon the stranger to attack,
    With cunning though he sat down by the track.

200

The swineherd followed, driving them away;
Then led Odysseus to his low abode,
And made him welcome, bidding him to stay;
Asking why he trod that lonely road.
He spoke about his master, so long gone,
And of his toils which fed those greedy curs,
And of those gifts his labours would have won
If his chief had come back from the wars.
Eumaeus then went down into the sties
And chose two swine and killed them for the spit.
He made that feast which hunger gratifies,
In halls or humble homes where strangers sit.
    And on the roast he sprinkled barley, white;
    Then mixed the honeyed wine which gives delight.

201

He sat and asked Odysseus to eat
That humble fare: young pigs, which slaves prepare.
He said: "The suitors have the richest meat,
That fattened hogs were sent up daily where
Those wastrels feasted richly, drawing wine
With wanton disregard from where it came."
He felt they must possess some news, malign,
About his lord, to dine so, with no shame.
As he spoke Odysseus ate the flesh
With grateful greed, so long denied good food,
And drank the wine but thought things dark and harsh
On how to spill ignoble suitor's blood.
    He asked Eumaus of the absent king
    In case his name he'd heard whilst journeying.

202

The swineherd said, with scorn, that many came
With tales about his master to the hall,
"Some were lies and no two were the same;
In tears his lady listened to them all,
Yet none convinced her or her noble son
That what they said about the king was true,
No doubt if you went there to tell them one
In handsome clothes, you would be listened to."
He said: "by now my master lies as bones,
Perhaps cast up on some shore, wrapped deep in sand;
Odysseus was his name, no more he roams
The sea grey path in search of his home land."
    He said he was ashamed to say that name
    Of one so kind to him, so great in fame.

203

The much enduring, noble lord replied
And said: "I tell you he will soon return
Before the waxing moon and changing tide,
And bring that vengeance which the suitors earn."
The swineherd doubted this could ever be
And said: "let's drink and speak of other things,
For when I hear that name of destiny
My heart feels grief, which sad remembrance brings,
For young Telamachus on his return,
For here with dire intent the suitors wait;
He went to Pylos of his sire to learn
If he comes back there waits an evil fate!
    Thus may end a race of noble fame
    And leave behind no lineage or name."

204

Eumaeus asked Odysseus whence he came?
Resourcefully, the sly lord made reply
Claiming that from Crete he'd gained his name,
From Castor and his concubine, wherebye
He came to lead a Cretan band in war.
Through that came fame and wealth, and then the call
To load his ships and man the sturdy oar,
To join the Grecian fleet so Troy might fall.
He said: "those days have passed, but looking now
On Autumn's stubble he might judge the grain,
And think on what he was when at the prow
He led his ships to victory and fame.
    For he was one who joyed in wars and spears
    And not those mundane tasks which weigh down years."

205

"Thus with Idomeneus then I went
To lead the Cretan ships to Ilium.
For ten long years we warred until Zeus sent
That evil day which caused them to succumb."
He spun a tale of how to Egypt then
He went with nine swift ships, adventuring;
But through the wanton looting of his men
He fell as bondsman to the Egyptian king.
For seven long years he stayed there gaining gold,
But then was gulled by a Phacian knave
Who offered passage so I might be sold,
Then through great Zeus his ship became a grave
 For those who crewed that ship to Libya,
 And left me drifting nine days on a spar.

206

Then on the tenth black night the rolling wave
Tossed me on the far Threspontian shore;
Pheidon the king a welcome shelter gave,
His son, my tired bones, to his palace bore.
Continuing the fiction then he said:
"That there he learned about the wanderer:
Odysseus—himself of course—who'd lead
A normal life, in far off Dodona."
Returning to himself as now disguised,
He said: then onto Dulchium he went
But by the crew had there been brutalised,
And stripped of garments, which the king had lent.
 Then dressed in rags they left him tied aboard,
 But breaking free, through surf, to shore he'd clawed.

207

He said: "the crew had searched, but gods were kind,
And hid him in the thicket of a wood,
Then led him to the swineherds hut to find
A welcome in that place where he now stood."
Eumaeus said: "the tale had stirred his heart
But he was not persuaded, none the less,
The gods had let his lord from war depart,
To vanish in the sea's great emptiness.
This shows they hate him utterly because:
He died without that glory which is due
To such a hero, by our funeral laws,
And with these tales come many such as you.
    Those stories once brought hope he would return
    But now just doubt and unbelief they earn."

208

Resourcefully Odysseus made reply—
"That they should make a covenant and see,
If that great lord returned, who could deny
That he spoke true, he then would claim a fee.
A cloak, a tunic, so he could return
To that place desired, but if he lied:
The wage of a deceiver he would earn
And for dissembling have his life denied!"
With irony Eumaeus said: "to slay
A guest, would bring him wealth and fame indeed;
Yet let us put such words and thoughts away,
For soon my men return, to rest and feed."
    Then as the world grew dark at evening time
    The other swineherds came and penned their swine.

209

Eumaeus called: "Bring in the best of boars
That we may feast this stranger who has come,
With sacrifice, according to our laws;"
And as he ordered, all those things were done.
In seven portions then he cut the meat,
One to the nymph and Hermes sacrificed,
And six for mortal men, set out to eat;
For his guest the long chine he had sliced,
Odysseus thanked him as that was the best;
Then with libations all sat down to dine,
Till sated at long last they went to rest;
Then darkness came, without the moon; malign,
    And Zeus sent rain to fall the whole night through,
    And gusting strong the cloud filled west wind blew.

210

Odysseus then spoke out with cunning words,
In trial to test the swineherd's good intent,
And told a boasting tale of how Greek lords
Beneath Troy's walls, in ambush, once were sent,
With him in third command, without a cloak.
Then during night the North wind sent down snow,
Thus bitter cold, Odysseus he woke,
And told him dawn would see him frozen, low.
That cunning lord then spoke to all around,
And said the gods sent warning in a dream:
Of danger! Which with help they might confound,
If one would run to ask their lord supreme,
    Great Agamemnon, if he would send aid;
    Young Thoas stood and that long journey made.

211

He left his purple cloak so he could run,
And I, till dawn, in that warm garment lay.
He said: "was I as then when strong and young,
Perhaps another cloak might come my way!"
Eumaeus took the point but said: "until
The son of great Odysseus returns,
The rags which you now wear must cloth you still,
At least for now your need a warm bed earns."
So there Odysseus slept yet ill content.
The swineherd slung his sword and took a spear,
And in a warm thick cloak to his boars went,
To guard them all from dangers which up-rear.
    He lay down, sheltered, with his white tusked boars,
    Under a hollow rock, beneath the stars.

Book 15

212

Athene went to wide Lacadaemon
To urge Telemachus should now return,
There in the palace porch with Nestor's son
She found him wakeful, anxious with concern.
While Menelaus slept she urged him back
And told him, rouse his host that he might go,
But warned him that the suitors might attack,
That he still faced great danger from his foe.
They waited now to kill him in his sleep
And in his hall they pressed increasing hard,
To prise his treasures from his mother's keep
With marriage bonds, designed to break her guard.
    She said: "Sail back, avoiding that wide strait
    Near Samos, where the evil suitors wait."

213

She urged him: "Sail by night as well as day
Avoiding land, until you reach your own;
Then send your comrades off without delay
To take their well earned rest within the town.
Yourself, go to the swineherd there to spend
The night in safety and when morning comes,
Send him with that welcome news to end
That fear which all her waking hours benumbs."
The goddess left; Telemachus then woke
And roused the son of Nestor from his sleep,
And with wingéd words to Peisistratus spoke
To say that now was time to cross the deep;
    Requesting that a chariot be brought
    To take him where his ship lay, in the port.

214

The son of Nestor urged that they delay
Till Menelaus came down with fitting gifts;
They rested then till golden dawn brought day,
Which from all eyes that blessing, slumber, lifts.
The king left fair tressed Helen sleeping still,
Telemachus then met him as he came
And told him he must leave or imperil
His legacy at home, debauched with shame.
The son of Atreus thus acquiesced
But asked he stay, till gifts were brought, and food;
Odysseus' son though urged on his request:
To leave in haste with heartfelt gratitude
    For all his father's friend had done for him
    Through days of feasting with that Spartan king.

215

Then Menelaus bade his good wife and slaves:
"At once, prepare repast for our young guest."
Then going to his treasure filled enclaves
Chose gifts to give him, of the very best:
A mixing bowl, two handled, there he chose,
Made by Hephaestus, silver chased with gold,
Given to him by one of the heroes
Phaedimus, who he had known of old.
Fair Helen set a bright robe in his hand,
Most beautiful of her embroideries;
Given for his bride when he at last should stand
Lord in his halls, blessed by all deities.
    These, Peisistratus took there from his lord,
    And gazed in wonder at that splendid hoard.

216

Then Menelaus led them to the hall
And maidens brought a golden pitcher down,
With water and a silver bowl so all
Could wash, and with a polished table drawn
Before them all they then sat down to eat;
A revered elder servant laid the food,
The son of Boethous carved off the meat;
All feasted then amongst that plenitude.
When all had had his fill of food and wine
Telemachus put horses to the yoke,
And Menelaus with parting words benign
Poured libation and his farewell spoke
  And asked that they should honoured greeting bring
  To ancient Nestor from great Sparta's king.

217

Telemachus said he would bear those words
To Ithaca, where he perhaps may find
His father in his halls, where faithful lords
Acknowledged him as king among his kind.
Then as he spoke a mighty eagle flew
On his right side, with fearsome talons round
A large tame goose of pure and pallid hue,
Which it had seized up from the palace ground.
Both then pondered what that sign could mean
Then Helen told them what the gods had shown:
Odysseus must now be near his deme!
Or from his wanderings even have come home
  To sow the seeds of evil to challenge
  The suitors all, and gain his sweet revenge.

218

He thanked her for the things she'd prophesised
And hoped that Zeus would grant that it would be;
Then his horses with the lash he tried,
To start them on their journey to the sea.
They left the city speeding to the plain,
And all day long, till sunset, they moved on.
They stayed with Diocles when darkness came,
In Pherae, until dawn's first light was won.
Then once more they sped onwards till they reached
The citadel of Pylos, where they stopped;
Telemachus then Nestor's son beseeched
That there beside his swift ship he be dropped.
    He knew that more delays would be impressed
    Upon him if he stayed there as a guest.

219

Thus, all those splendid gifts were stowed aboard,
And Peisistratus urged that he should leave
With all his comrades, and the treasure hoard,
For he knew Nestor then would sorely grieve,
That he had lost the chance to act as host
To the son of one he honoured still,
Yet now he paused upon that wild sea coast
His duties to Athene to fulfil.
Then, when he'd poured libations came a man
Called Theoclymenus, a fugitive,
Who said from black fate's furies he now ran
And begged for passage as a poor plaintive.
    Telemachus with noble heart replied,
    That he would never push such pleas aside.

220

He bade the stranger board his well made ship
And took his spear of bronze and laid it down.
He then told Theoclymenus to sit,
Thus to a couch astern the guest was shown.
His men then raised the mast and fixed the stays
And flashing eyed Athene sent a wind,
Which pushed the swift ship through the grey sea ways
Past Crouni and Chalcis as was destined.
They sailed till daylight faded at Pheae,
Then on past splendid Elis swift they sped
And to the shear cliffed islands made their way,
Evading death and capture on they fled.
    Well knowing that the suitors lay in wait
    Telemachus then pondered on his fate.

221

Far off though great Odysseus took wine
And ate his fill with all the swineherds there,
And then replete at last he thought it time
To try his host for kind intent, and care.
He said that in the morning he might go
Into the city, staying there to beg;
He asked for guides to lead him down below
In hope of water and a loaf of bread.
He said he might move on to the great house
To take his news to wise Penelope;
Then join the suitors, watching them carouse,
And carve them meat and serve wine, equally.
    He said he had no equal in those tasks
    Of carvery, or broaching well filled casks.

222

Then, deeply moved, Eumaeus made reply:
That if he went amid that wanton throng
Their lawless ways must mean that he would die,
For all their serving men were fair and young;
Well clad in cloaks, with hair and faces sleek.
They tend the tables filled with bread and meat
Served wine and brought all things their masters seek.
He said: "stay safe with us and this fate cheat!"
He told him: "when Telemachus comes home
That lord himself will clothe you fittingly,
And send you on, wherever you would roam."
He urged: "Please stay amid our company!"
    Odysseus thus had tested those around,
    And by his cunning loyal friends had found.

223

He praised Eumaeus for his kindness then,
For now at last his wanderings had ceased;
He told them: "nothing worse can come to man
Than that curse from which I am released."
Odysseus asked him of his parents who
He had left, approaching their old age;
The swine herd said: "Though restful death was due
His father trod still on this earthly stage;
In mourning though, for his dead wife and son.
That lady, pining for him, died of grief;
She lived in sorrow till her end was won,
And old Laertes prays for death's relief."
    Eumaeus said: "With her child, Climene
    He had been raised in days long gone, carefree."

224

He said: "When both had reached youth's lovely prime,
To Same she had gone to be a bride;
Whilst he was given a cloak and tunic fine
And sent, where still the herdsmen's boys reside.
He knew she'd loved him almost as her own
And he lacked nothing through his god blessed toils;
Yet she had died; and now her life had flown
He brooded as the suitors took their spoils."
Odysseus asked him then of his own lands
And by what means he'd come into this isle;
Eumaeus said: "From Syria, which stands
Above Ortygia, through a woman's guile.
　　His father Ctessius there ruled as king;
　　The land was fair and rich in everything.

225

He said Phoenicians came, in ships, to trade
And found a female slave there, of their race;
One of the crew sweet love to her soon made,
And asked her who she was and from what place.
She said from Sidon rich in bronze she'd come;
Seized by Taphian pirates and then sold.
He offered to return her to her home
To see her parents who still lived, though old.
She told him then, through barter, fill his ship,
And then when ready send, concealed, the word,
For her to come, then secretly she'd slip
Down to the port with gold, and bring aboard
　　Her noble master's child whom they might sell
　　For some great price, in lands where strangers dwell.

226

She swore them all to silence till that time
Their trade was done and they prepared to leave;
For then a man must come with secret sign
That she must join them, and their hosts deceive.
Thus on that day a man well versed in guile
Brought up an amber necklace strung with gold,
And gave the sign with nod and knowing smile,
Of treachery, which told her to be bold.
She seized three golden cups left by the men,
And took the child by hand and led him down
To their ship, which swiftly embarked then
And bore me off far from my home and town.
    For six days then we sailed with god sent winds
    Yet on the seventh she died, for she had sinned.

227

Artemis, the archer, struck her dead,
She fell into the hold like some killed bird
Which thudded down onto its earthen bed,
Her corpse was swiftly, mid the waves, interred,
To feed the seals and fish, with no respect.
I was left alone without my nurse
With heart made sore through darkest fate's neglect;
I feared then what new woes it might disburse.
The god though smiled and brought me to this isle,
Where great Laertes bought me with his wealth.
Since then I've lived here in my long exile
With food and wine made strong, and in good health.
    The swine-herds tale thus moved Odysseus,
    Who said: "That good and evil come from Zeus!"

228

They then set down to sleep, and at next dawn
Telemachus arrived on that fair shore;
He feasted all the crew and then made known
His plans to all those of his loyal corps.
He told them: "Row the ship to harbour now,
For I must find the herdsmen of my lands;
Then view my fields, till passing hours allow
Me to come with wine and rich viands."
God like Theoclymenus had doubt,
Asking to which house he now should go.
Telemachus said: "Better stay without
Your mother's house; but then from Apollo
    A sign appeared: a hawk, which clasped a dove,
    This showed Odysseus' son was loved by Jove.

229

Then noble Theoclymenus was sure
That all was well, by omen prophesised;
He knew Telemachus surely would endure
Those dangers which the suitors had devised.
He took the young man's hand in fealty,
And praised his line as kingly and supreme,
The young lord told Peiraeus: "Faithfully
Take my guest homeward, to my waiting deme."
He went on board and bade them all, embark!
He donned his sandals, then took up his spear
And left the ship, whilst they let loose that barque
And sailed down to the city in good cheer.
    Telemachus, with urgency, strode on
    Until the worthy swineherd's hut was won.

Book 16

230

Back in the herdsman's hut at early dawn
A fire was kindled, new, to cook some food;
With dogs and swine out in the early morn,
The herdsmen moved among their feasting brood.
When Telemachus came near the dogs all fawned,
And did not bark as though some slayer came.
Odysseus heard the footsteps, then he warned
That this must be some person known by name
To thus be greeted by those savage hounds,
And as he said this in the doorway stood
That sight of joy, which eye and mind astounds,
Telemachus, grown tall, near full manhood.
 Eumaeus rose to greet him as a son,
 With tears of welcome, from those old eyes won.

231

The swine herd spoke warm words in great delight
Which welcomed his young lord from dangers past;
Telemachus then asked him of the plight
Of his dear mother, noble, and steadfast.
The swineherd said: "The suitors she withstood,
Though at night she wept for those thought lost,
And through long days could see no hope or good
For still the suitors wished, her, to accost."
Odysseus then arose as his fine son
Came near; he offered that young man his seat.
His heir then thanked him for that kindness done
But told him, sit, while they took drink and meat.
 The swineherd brought green brushwood and a fleece
 And all sat down to eat their homely feast.

232

When satisfied Telemachus enquired
From where this stranger sat with them had come?
The swineherd said: "From Crete and he desired
To be of service to Odysseus' son."
The young man said: "As yet I have no means
To take a supplicant into those halls
As all the wealth therein is yet the Queens,
And she is wooed still by the suitors all."
He said though he would cloth him fittingly
And give him sandals and a two edged sword,
Then send him onwards, well equipped and free
Or he could stay here of his own accord.
  He could not to the palace let him go
  As strife might come and they might lay him low.

233

Odysseus then answered: "Noble friend,
On hearing of the suitors wantonness,
I wonder now why none with you defend
Your wealth, and give you vengeance and redress."
Telemachus replied: "Through single line
My house is formed and I have brothers none,
Nor uncles as by Cronos' law, divine,
My father also was an only son.
Now foes past counting occupy my halls,
Lords of Ithaca and all the isles;
They come to woo my mother but she stalls,
Avoiding marriage by her skilful wiles;
  Neither can she end the suitors waste
  Thus year replaces year in vile disgrace."

234

Telemachus then bade the stranger—go!
To tell his mother he was safe and well,
And then return when he had eased her woe,
For he would stay now where poor swineherds dwell.
Eumaeus said: "That in the selfsame way
He should seek Laertes with the news
For mourning holds him since you went away;
He waits till death his failing flesh subdues."
The young lord said: "that we must let him be
Yet tell my mother, swift, to send her maid,
In secret, with the news then we will see
That old Laertes' spirit will not fade."
    Thus he sent the swineherd on his way,
    With words of hope to lift such long dismay.

235

And as he went Athene then drew near
In woman's form and stood against the gate
Odysseus, only, saw her shape appear
And with her eyebrows saw her indicate,
That he must come to hear what she would say.
He crossed the courtyard, passed the wall, alone;
The dogs knew she was there, yet in dismay
They cowered low within the swineherd's home.
She kept her presence from his noble son,
But then the goddess said he must reveal
His secret to him, and when that was done
Those two could plan in vengeful death to deal,
    And spill the suitor's blood, with lust and hate,
    For years of insult to his great estate.

236

Athene touched him with her golden wand
And made him tall once more, in youthful bloom,
Clad in garments, spell wrought by her hand,
She gave him strength to bring the suitors down.
When she left Odysseus went inside;
Telemachus then looked at him, amazed;
He thought that by some god his eyes were tried,
And thus beguiled, upon that changed form gazed.
His much enduring, noble, father spoke
Revealing in that moment his true name,
And from his eyes a single tear then broke
That now his dear young son he would regain.
    Telemachus though doubted what he said,
    Believing him some guileful god instead.

237

Odysseus reassured him saying how
This was all Athene's cunning spell;
She'd made him as a beggar, seeming low,
And then released him from that threadbare shell.
So saying he sat down next to his son
Who threw his arms about his sire and wept;
And from both eyes hot tears of joy were won,
Loud wailing from the throats of both men leapt,
Like those of eagles country folk had robbed
Of fledglings, helpless, taken from the nest,
Their tears fell down as crying voices throbbed,
And hearts, near broken, mended in each breast.
    The weeping may have carried on past dusk
    But son to father then a question thrust!

238

Telemachus then asked, which sailor race
Had brought him down the seaways to this shore;
Odysseus said he'd come back by the grace
Of the Phaeacians with his treasure store,
Which now was laid up near the Naiad's caves.
He said with great Athene's aid he came
To plan the slaying of those suitor slaves,
He asked his son to list them each by name;
With numbers known, to thus decide if two
Would be enough to slaughter all of them,
His son though listed many, not a few,
With herald, minstrel, and some serving men.
    He knew his father's battle skills were great
    But asked that other's helped them deal death's fate.

239

Odysseus said two helpers he could name:
Great Zeus and fair Athene set on high,
These would be with them when the conflict came,
When, stained by greed the suitors, dead, would lie.
He said though now he needed to give thought
On who might aid them in that mortal strife,
When those vile lords found what dishonour brought
And each paid for his insults with his life.
He then said: "Go at daybreak to our house
And join the suitor's company and wait,
Keep your council while they all carouse,
Then, as a beggar I will pass your gate,
    Led by the swineherd, clad in rags, I'll come
    To measure them and see what might be done."

240

He said: "Despite their scorn you must endure
If I am pelted or they drag me in,
Seek to dissuade them yet you can be sure
They will not hear, for doom they soon must win.
And when Athene, rich in council, says
To my mind, a signal I will give;
Then you must take all weapons from their bays
And hide them in a store, be secretive.
For when the suitors miss their arms and ask,
You must beguile them saying they are laid
Out of the smoke, which with its grimy mask
Has poured befoulment on each shaft and blade,
    And tell them they are moved should come a time
    They reach for them in anger, hot with wine."

241

He said: "Though leave behind two swords and spears,
There with ox-hide shields which we might grasp
When we rush up, for soon the conflict nears;
Zeus and Athene aid us in our task!
They will beguile those mortals while we act,
But all of this in secret must be done,
For none must know about our deadly pact,
Laertes, nor my wife, nor anyone.
For I must of my household, all, make trial,
To sift the loyal ones from those who'll pay:
With lives, that they upon the suitors smile,
And serve their lusts and greed without dismay."
    Telemachus though said those trials should wait,
    For they must stop the waste of his estate.

242

Then while they spoke his ship to harbour came,
And all the beauteous gifts were sent to lie
Up in the house of Clytius whose fame,
And noble heart none ever would deny.
They also sent a herald to the hall
To carry word to wise Penelope,
To stop those fears which caused her tears to fall,
When dwelling on her great son's destiny.
The herald and the noble swineherd met
On that same errand with its message clear,
Eumaeus spoke though in secret,
The herald spoke aloud that all might hear.
    The suitors became downcast at his news,
    And broodingly went from the hall to muse.

243

Then Eurymachus, first amongst them spoke,
About this great deed, insolently done!
Well covered by some god's protecting cloak,
Odysseus' son had through all dangers won.
He then proposed they send a swift black ship
And those who lay in ambush there, recall;
Yet, scarce that word had passed his scheming lip
When Amphinomous turned round from the wall
And saw their comrades to the harbour come,
And laughing said: "No message needs be sent,
For by some means they know, and have come home:
They could not catch this youth or cause his end."
    They rose and went down to the shore to ask,
    What stopped their comrades in that murderous task?

244

In secret convocation all were met
And then Antinous said: "Day by day
Our watchmen on the windy heights were set
In constant search above the sea lanes, grey,
When darkness came they then sailed out to wait,
In case the ship they sought, at night, might try
To save Telemachus from his dark fate,
But all their evil schemes had gone awry."
He said: "Come now, we must devise a plan
To bring down woeful death upon his head
Before he rouses his Achaean clan,
And tells them of our scheme to see him dead.
    We must seize him as he homeward speeds
    Before they learn about our evil deeds."

245

Amphinomous though spoke among them all,
He led those suitors from rich Dulchium,
And said: "If by their hands this youth will fall,
The god's revenge to all of them might come,
For he now dreaded royal stock to slay,
Thus they should ascertain the Olympian's will."
This pleased them and they rose and went their way
Up to their host's great hall, yet bent on ill.
Penelope had learned about the threat
From Medon, a fair herald, who heard all;
Thus near the door post, in her veil, she met
Antinous and went on to recall
    How his father turned a fugitive,
    And how her husband's help had let him live.

246

She railed against him for the schemes he'd wrought
To kill her son, and mire their noble names;
Then Eurymachus, answering her, sought
To calm her, and deflect from them, the shame.
He said that while he lived he would defend
Her son, for he was dearest of all men,
And he would, with his spear, to Hades send
All who tried to harm her dear one then,
And through his words the noble lady cheered:
(In secret her son's death he much desired.)
Thus released from all that which was feared
She went up to her chamber and retired.
    A while she spent in tears, sore wracked by sighs,
    Until Athene brought sleep to her eyes.

247

At evening, with the swine herd near returned,
Athene struck Odysseus with her wand;
Then once more to an aged wretch he turned,
As through her skill the beggar's rags he'd donned.
With supper set the son asked old Eumaeus
What news of the proud suitors he had heard,
He said: "Their evils he would not discuss,
But hurried back here when the Queen had word."
He said, though, one thing with his eyes he'd seen:
"A ship with well armed men came harbouring!"
Those words then caused the young lord's eyes to gleam,
That fate should near their spears those traitors bring.
    They set to feasting, then with cheerful minds
    They sought that rest which just men's labour finds.

Book 17

248

When early dawn appeared, low, in the sky
Telemachus then bound his sandals on,
And took his spear and told his old ally,
The swine-herd, that to town he must be gone.
He told him he must take the stranger there
So he might beg his food and then be left;
Odysseus played his part and feigned no care
Affirming: he preferred the beggar's craft,
To labour, here, among those herds of swine;
When warmed by the good fire he would go down.
Telemachus then left that high confine
And journeyed to his mother's hall, alone.
    As he swift walked he brooded on his plan,
    To slay the suitors, sparing not one man.

249

He came up to the hall and set in place
His spear against a pillar, near the door;
He crossed the threshold then came face to face
With his old nurse, who set chairs on the floor.
Eurycleia greeted him with tears,
Then, round him gathered all the palace maids
They kissed him then, for all their mounting fears
Had vanished as the dark in dawn's light fades.
Out from her chamber came Penelope,
Like Aphrodite, golden, she appeared,
Or Artemis; her dearest son to see;
Through sobs of joy she said that she had feared
    That never more to her he would return,
    From Pylos and his dangerous sojourn.

250

About his father then she asked for news
But he put off her questions and advised
That she retire and his reply excuse,
As he had just escaped that death devised
By those who'd lain in wait for his return.
He said that she should bathe then sacrifice
To all the gods in hope that she might earn
Their favours by her prayers: a blessed device.
He said that he must now depart to bring
A stranger he had met, up to their hall;
She heard his words but said in turn, nothing,
And swift retired to pray to the gods: all.
    Telemachus then left with spear in hand
    And two swift dogs, to start what he had planned.

251

He went down fast to the assembly place,
And all the people wondered as he came;
Athene had around him spread such grace
That with respect the suitors spoke his name.
But he kept clear though of their greatest throng
And went where Mentor sat and Antiphus,
And Halisthernes, going thus among
Those friends of old of great Odysseus.
Then spear-famed Peiraeus drew near,
Who'd led the stranger to the meeting place;
Telemachus then saw his guest appear
And went to greet him with his lordly grace.
    Peiraeus at once spoke of the gold
    Which Telemachus gave to him to hold.

252

He then replied: "That crew are plotting still,
Thus better that my treasure stays with you,
But If I sow the seeds of death and kill
These wastrels, you may then return my due."
The much tried stranger, then, the prince led home,
And there they bathed and feasted till replete;
His mother asked: what of her lord was known?
And with tears did hopeful news entreat.
Telemachus then told her of his quest,
Where he'd journeyed and which kings he'd seen,
On fair Calypso's isle, the son confessed,
His father languished, captive to that queen.
  Then with rich gifts and all his searching done,
  With god sent winds, his home isle he had won.

253

God like Theoclymenus then spoke,
In prophecy: "That even now, 'the King'
Roamed abroad unknown to those foul folk,
And learned how best deservéd death to bring
Down on the suitors, of this he was sure:
From that bird, which as an omen came,
This by all the gods I here adjure:
Their end must come, through death's all cleansing flame!"
The Queen then said: "Might all this be fulfilled,
Then many gifts will shower around your head;"
Yet while she spoke the suitors played and drilled
With spear and discus, waiting to be fed.
  Then when the flocks came in a herald bade
  Them come to slaughter, that a feast be made.

254

Odysseus and the swineherd made their way
Down to the city by the rugged path;
Eumaeus felt it better that he stay,
Yet must obey, or face his master's wrath.
Thus dressed in rags and with a pouch, much holed,
And with a staff to lean on, both set out.
Then near the town they found a fountain, old,
Used by the people, where fresh waters spout;
Nymphs had made it for them long ago.
Now, by their altar in a poplar grove
They met Melanthius, a haughty fellow,
Who to the suitors feast, his fat goats drove,
    He reviled them as he passed them by
    And aimed a kick hard at Odysseus' thigh—

255

But he stayed firm, unmoving, at the blow
And pondered, if this goatherd he should kill?
He stood and took those insults, just for now,
Yet asked the gods his vengeful prayers—fulfil.
Melanthius then spoke up: "This dog talks,"
And vowed some day to sell him as a slave,
And cursed in hope that foul death's shadow stalks
Odysseus' son, then onward went that knave
And quickly found the palace of the king,
Then sat near Eurymachus as he ate.
Out from the hall came sounds of revelling
As swineherd and his guest approached the gate.
    Phemius, inside, sang with his lyre,
    And odours of roast meat rose from the fire.

256

Odysseus clasped Eumaeus by the hand
And feigned to recognise that noble hall,
The swineherd asked if he now entry planned
Or would wait, while he prepared them all.
Odysseus asked that he should go before
Him to the suitors, while he waited here,
For he had suffered blows on waves, in war,
And would endure outside and have no fear.
Then as they spoke, an old dog laid outside,
Raised his head up as those strangers neared
And pricked his ears as those two men he eyed
For this was Argus who Odysseus reared,
    The steadfast dog, who'd waited twenty years,
    He sniffed and looked, unsure, through rheumy tears.

257

In days gone by the young man took this hound
To hunt wild goats and hares and leaping deer,
But now he lay neglected on the ground
Amid that dung, which heaped up, was left near
The doors, until the slaves took it away
To scatter on the fields so crops would grow.
Now neglected, full of ticks he lay,
But he knew well his master neared him now.
He wagged his tail and dropped his ears to greet
His owner, but no longer had the strength
To move and sit before his master's feet.
Odysseus looked aside, yet spoke at length,
    For he had turned to wipe aside a tear,
    He said how strange this fine old dog lay here.

258

Eumaeus said to him: "The dog was owned
By someone who had died in foreign lands;
When young he had no equal as he roamed,
Hunting through thick woods or down swept sands,
But now beset by fleas the old dog lies:
Ignored, because his master is no more."
But joy of recognition filled those eyes
As now Odysseus neared him at the door,
For in that twentieth year his master came,
And noble Argus knew that he could end,
His task was done, he thus gave up the flame
Of life which had sustained that faithful friend.
    Thus with black death, in joy, the old dog went
    His master had returned, he was content.

259

Then the swineherd strode into the hall;
Telemachus, the godlike, saw him first,
And quickly made a sign with which to call
Him over, there to eat and quench his thirst.
Close after him Odysseus entered in
Dressed as a beggar leaning on his stick,
In woeful state, his threadbare rags worn thin,
Looking like an ancient weary rustic.
He sat down on the ash-wood just within
The threshold, leant against the cypress door,
Telemachus then called Eumaeus to him,
To give him bread and meat for one so poor.
    He sent the food with word: "When such need came,
    That he should beg from all there with no shame."

260

Odysseus thanked the squire who brought him food
And set it on his pouch so he might eat,
He sent thanks to that prince of noble blood
For hunger banished by that food and meat.
Thus, while the minstrel sang he slowly ate,
But when he ceased the suitors uproar raised;
Athene came and urged he circulate
Among them, begging, with his hands upraised.
They gave, and marvelled, asking who he was
Whilst he weighed up the better and the worst;
How they ranked there mattered not, because:
Each one by Athene was now cursed!
    Melanthius, the goatherd, spoke to all
    And said he knew that stranger to their hall.

261

He said: "Eumaeus, the swineherd, brought him there
But did not know which city gave him birth,"
Antinous then asked: "Why did he dare
To bring this beggar for there was no dearth
Of vagabonds, who came to spoil their feasts.
Was it not enough that suitors came
To revel and devour his master's beasts!"
Eumaeus said that noble should feel shame
For those words, mean spirited, which broke
The laws of hospitality which bound
Them welcome all, both skilled and beggar folk,
That in him harshest words were always found.
    'All there once Odysseus had served'—
    Telemachus at once that outburst curbed.

262

He said Antinous would use harsh words
Through habit to provoke in men vile rage,
Explaining that the will of Zeus affords
A welcome to all there, to lord and slave.
He then accused that lofty prince of greed,
And said that he would rather eat than give!
Then all the other suitors there, indeed,
Gave the beggar food that he might live.
Antinous seized the footstool near his feet—
Odysseus told him then a mocking tale
Of how he'd gone to Egypt with his fleet,
And how the gods had made his mission fail.
    Wanton pillage by his savage men
    Had called down Zeus' swift revenge on them.

263

Then as a slave, through Cyprus, he'd come hence
Dressed as a beggar, having lost his lands;
He asked for food as some small recompense
As others had in past times from his hands;
These were never sent away till filled.
Antinous replied: "Their feast he spoiled!"
And asked: "What god this bane upon us willed?"
Then told him to stand off lest anger boiled
Within his head, for this would bring him pain.
Odysseus then came back with quick retort
"That he had much, yet would not give a grain,
A single grain of salt, such was his sort!
    Antinous in fury that he dared
    Reproach him thus, with angry glances, glared!

264

He threw the footstool then, with ire, towards
Odysseus, whom, with great force it then struck,
But like a rock he stood unmoving, hard,
As that foul missile smote him in his back.
He shook his head in silence pondering,
Revenge, yet to his place he went to sit,
But next, among the suitors, spoke out wondering:
"What sort of man would thus a beggar hit?"
He said: "If such, the gods and furies guard,
May doom upon Antinous soon fall."
That lord replied: "Sit still or in the yard
Go out to eat away from this great hall,
    For fear the young men drag you from the house
    And strip your skin, whilst we inside carouse."

265

Those words drew indignation from them all
Which that proud youth, Antinous, condemned;
They warned him for such deeds, death's hand may fall;
Such were the laws which suppliants defend.
Yet that dark prince ignored those righteous words—
Close by, Telemachus held back his rage
But pondered blood-revenge amid those lords
And ways his father's hurt there to assuage.
Penelope, above, heard of the deed
And prayed the gods might strike the culprit dead,
The old nurse Eurynome took the lead
In praying that to Hades he be led.
    The queen though said: "Those men are evil all,
    I pray the hand of fate will on them fall."

266

She said: "Antinous, though was the worst,
And to black-death compared that evil one;
A guest there seeking alms by him was cursed
And from his rage a hurtful blow was won.
She called the noble swineherd to her side
And told Eumaeus: "bid the stranger come
That I may greet and ask him to confide
In me his news of Laertes' lost son."
The swineherd told her that well woven tale
Which hid the secret of her lord's return,
And yet gave hope that soon his ship would sail—
The suitors then their fated deaths would earn.
    Penelope said: "Call him to this place
    That he might tell me all things, face to face.

267

Yet leave the suitors to their revelling,
For through the absence of my noble lord,
They despoil our wealth and nothing bring
In payment for the wasting of our hoard,
And should our king return to claim his lands
Vengeance on those wastrel soon will fall,
Delivered from his, and his proud son's strong hands."
At those wise words, down in the feasting hall,
Telemachus her son sneezed out aloud;
She laughed gently, saying that this showed
That death for certain now must soon enshroud
Antinous, and all that evil crowd.
    She said: "Now quick to me this stranger bring
    That I might learn of all his journeying."

268

Thus to Odysseus the swineherd went
To give the message from Penelope,
That lord though asked: "for now she should relent,
And wait till sunset came and he was free.
He sought the suitor's insolence to shun,
Avoiding blows and insults from that crew;
Then in the evening he would surely come
And sitting near her tell her all he knew."
Eumaeus took his message to the queen
Who recognised the wisdom of his plan,
She said that she would wait for him, serene,
Amid her maids, till eventide began.
    Eumaeus then went off to tend his swine
    And left the suitors to their food and wine.

Book 18

269

There came a public beggar from the town
A braggart named Arnaeus, known for greed,
Yet as Irus by all there was known,
For he ran errands when some lord had need.
Odysseus, in his own hall! He reviled,
And tried to move him off, for his own sake,
And with low threats his personage defiled,
The mighty lord replied with words of hate,
Advising that the vagrant should desist
And share that threshold as all beggars should,
If not his lips might feel an angry fist,
His breast and face would redden with spilled blood.
    Irus though piled insult upon threat,
      A bully's words, which he would soon regret.

270

He said Odysseus was a glutton, who,
Spoke glibly, like an ancient kitchen maid,
That evil blows from him would soon be due,
With threats like these he filled his foul tirade.
The blowhard thought, with menace, to hold sway
And this would make Odysseus back down,
Yet Irus would find out to his dismay:
That words come cheap, and easily are thrown.
Antinous then heard the two and laughed,
And urged that they should set the beggars on,
To see if deeds could with proud words be matched
With just reward for whom that contest won.
    A goats-skin pouch and always there, a seat,
      To join the suitors in their nightly feast.

271

With crafty mind Odysseus spoke out then,
To say that he was old and full of woe,
He drew a promise thus from all of them
That none should aid the braggart with a blow,
Which thrown would favour Irus with a win.
All gave the oath, Telemachus then spoke
To guarantee it so they might begin,
All swore that none that promise would revoke.
Odysseus girded up his rags to fight:
Revealing powerful thighs and shoulders broad,
With muscled chest and mighty arms in sight
The suitors murmured praise, all in accord.
  Athene then drew near and magnified
  His limbs to greater size, stood at his side.

272

Irus heard the suitor's words of praise
And with a quaking heart he, slow, prepared;
With trembling limbs and filled with dread malaise,
Concerned that in the fight he'd not be spared.
Antinous upbraided him and said:
"You tremble now before an older man
Overcome by woe, by hunger led,
To prove himself before this noble clan.
If it comes to pass that you should lose
In a black ship I'll send you as a slave
In chains to king Echtus, to taste abuse,
With ears and nose cut off, sent to your grave.
  He will feed your genitals to dogs,
  To propiate your insult to the gods."

273

Yet greater trembling, seized poor Irus' limbs
As he was lead into the ring to fight;
Odysseus pondered whether for his sins
To strike him hard, depriving him of life,
Or with a lighter blow to lay him low,
This, to him then, seemed the better course,
For then the evil suitors would not know
What deadly skills his might would soon enforce.
Odysseus thus struck Irus on the neck
Beneath the ear, hard, staving in the bones;
The red blood flowed as downward fell that wreck
Who kicked the ground and gnashed and gave out moans.
    The suitors howled with laughter, well amused,
    To see that fool and braggart so abused.

274

Odysseus dragged him out, up to the gates,
And leaned him there with staff thrust in his hand,
He told him: "Here your future duty waits
To scare off dogs and swine which roam this land."
He hung about his neck his wretched pouch
And left him there, and went back in the hall,
Then mid the suitors sat down on his couch,
And he was greeted merrily by all.
They said: "May Zeus fulfil your hearts desire!"
This made Odysseus glad, for he alone
Saw in those words an omen dark and dire,
Which told that soon to Death they must atone
    For all their greed and insults to his line,
    Which soon would end by aid of one divine.

275

They gave him the goat pouch and two fine loaves,
Amphinomous then pledged a cup of gold
And said: "May you receive what fate behoves:
Let this be happiness when you grow old."
Odysseus with a shrewd head made reply
And said: "You seem to be a prudent man
As was your father: Nisus, even I
Have heard about the fame of his great clan.
Yet perhaps you should take warning from my words
As justice for men's evils waits for all,
For lawless ways will bring their just rewards
And lawless things I see, within this hall.
    The suitors, waste, and foul dishonour bring,
    Unto the wife of Ithaca's great king."

276

Odysseus spoke in warning: "Vengeance comes!"
He said: "It would be better now to leave,
For he who stays to waiting death succumbs,
None may avoid his hand, or fate deceive."
Amphinomus went on, with heaving heart,
With head bowed low his instincts boding ill,
His ending neared yet he could not depart,
Marked out for slaughter by Athene's will.
The goddess put a notion in the mind
Of wise Penelope that she should go
Amid the suitors all, and make them blind
With passion which from lust and greed would flow.
    She said to Eurynome, laughing loud,
    That she would go amid those suitors proud.

277

She said, though first that she must see her son
To tell him not to mix with that vile crew,
Which spoke to him with honour, every one,
But meant him ill hereafter, she well knew.
Her housekeeper advised that this she do,
Yet told her not to go with tear stained cheeks,
Counselling, her beauty she renew
Before descending mid that noisome clique.
Penelope replied that she could not
Wash herself, or use anointing oil,
For queenly beauty, which the gods allot,
Had vanished when Odysseus left his soil.
    She said: "Send Hippodameia to me
    And with her the fair maid Autonoe."

278

Eurynome went to bid them come;
Athene then brought pleasant slumber down
Around the queen and when sweet sleep was won,
Like Cythera who wears the splendid crown
Used ambrosial beauty on her face,
Made her taller, statelier in form,
With pure white skin and limbs imbued with grace.
She then awoke as radiant as the dawn,
And left that upper chamber with her maids,
And in her shining veil stood at the door;
There; when the suitors saw her, those proud blades
Prayed to lie beside her evermore.
    All were drenched in lust with knees grown weak,
    Yet none would gain that queen which all hearts seek.

279

She spoke there to her staunch and noble son,
And told him of those fears which held her then,
Upbraiding him for all that violence done
To the stranger by those bestial men.
He said: "Her anger he well understood
But all around were men of evil thoughts,
Though they'd planned to see the stranger bleed
Irus had been felled by his onslaught."
He wished by Zeus the suitors could feel shame.
Within the house, for now all were subdued;
Eurymachus towards them, slyly, came
And spoke about that beauty which bestrewed
    That noble queen with favours, rich, sublime,
    She moved and stood, and talked, as one divine.

280

Penelope then wisely made reply:
"That all her beauty had the gods destroyed
On that day Odysseus left for Troy,
Since then her life with sorrow was employed.
When he embarked he said that some would die
And never more return to hold their wives;
For some must fall when spears and arrows fly,
On Troy's plain must lie those lost Argives."
She said: "they should be mindful of her state,
And if they wished to woo her they should bring
Rich gifts to win this lady as their mate,
And not devour the wealth of her lost king."
    Her speech invited gifts from those foul lords
    And made Odysseus glad to hear her words.

281

Antinous then spoke amongst them all,
And said: "those of the Greeks who wished to bring
Some gift, should bring them to this noble hall,
But she must then choose one of them as king
And they would stay there till she chose the best."
The suitors heard his words and all were glad,
Each sent his herald homeward on that quest
To bring the finest thing which each man had.
Antinous himself gave her a dress,
Richly wrought, with brooches made of gold;
Eurymachus, a necklace to impress
With amber beads, which like the bright sun glowed.
    Eurydamus—ear-rings from his squire,
    Each with three fine jewels which burned like fire.

282

Each Achaean brought her gifts divine,
Then with her handmaids called, she swift retired;
Thus the suitors turned to song and wine
And waited till the last of day expired.
When dark night came they set three braziers up
Within the hall, with torches all around,
To give them light by which they long could sup
And kindling ready, scattered on the ground.
Then as the maidens set flame to the wood
Odysseus told them: "upstairs they should go,
And sat beside their mistress, there they should
Work their wool as he made light below.
    For if they feast till dawn I will endure
    And keep the hall well lit you may be sure."

283

At his words the maids began to laugh
And worst of all was fair cheeked Melantho,
Who scolded him, on all those girl's behalf
And said the wine had made his wits turn slow.
She said: "if he persisted one might rise
And beat him till the blood streamed from his head,
Not an Irus, who, now outside lies,
But one from mid the suitors, nobly bred."
This was the child who Dolius begot
And who Penelope reared as her own,
Yet she that kindness easily forgot
And did not sorrow for her now, full grown,
 But slept with Eurymachus whom she loved
 And cared not if she knew or disapproved.

284

Odysseus looked with anger on the maid
And said: "Telemachus, he now would seek
To tell him of this bitch who disobeyed
So he might with a sword blood-vengeance wreak,
And hack her limb from limb, "and with those words
That maiden ran in terror from the hall.
Then the stranger went among those lords
To tend the torches, bringing light to all.
Athene though stirred up the suitors there
To speak with insults, stoking up his ire
This caused Odysseus' anger, hot, to flare,
Thus in his heart burned dark revenge's fire.
 Polybus' son, Eurymachus began
 With jibes to bring forth mirth from that foul clan.

285

He mocked him for the torch-glare showed his head
Shine brightly in the light, devoid of hair;
He asked the stranger: "would he serve, if fed,
Upon his farm to labour through the year."
Asking: "would he rather beg and skulk?"
Resourcefully, Odysseus made reply:
And said: "That in those fields he may well sulk
If his fine boasts he could not justify,
When, they with scythes cut hay till darkness came,
All would find who was the better one,
Or when ploughing saying who could claim
That he the greatest acreage had done;
 And if in war they stood with shield and spear,
 They would see who battled without fear.

286

Odysseus called him insolent and cruel,
For taunting someone caught in hunger's vice;
Soon, one might come to end their foul misrule,
And waste for which swift death would be the price.
Eurymachus grew angry in his heart
And spoke with wrath and looked with glowering brows,
He said: "from wine those babbling words must start,"
Then picked a stool up, growling threatening vows.
Then Odysseus, weighing up that frown,
Sat at lord Amphinomous' rear;
Eurymachus with his fist knocked down
One who poured out wine there, standing near.
 The man crouched down and groaned, upon the floor;
 The startled suitors shouted in uproar.

287

They spoke about the stranger who had brought
Such tumult where before there had been joy;
To brawl because of beggars of that sort
Would revels end—cause appetites to cloy.
Telemachus then said: "they must be moved
By some strange god and now they should go home;"
Amphinomous, those lordly words approved
And said: "the time to leave our feast has come."
The words he spoke were pleasing to them all,
Thus, Mulius poured wine out for those men
And with libations made, they left the hall
And each, content, went willing homewards then.
    The stranger though, they left, for he had come
    To his own house to stay with his great son.

Book 19

288

Thus, with Athene, great Odysseus planned
The slaying of the suitors in his hall;
Then to his valiant son he made demand:
That he must gather up the weapons all;
And tell the wastrel suitors, if they ask,
The shining bronze is all befouled by grime,
That fear of angry words impels your task
Should they reach for blades when hot with wine.
He then called forth the nurse and said to her:
"Shut the serving women in their rooms,"
Eurycleia said: "He must have care
To guard his father's treasures and heirlooms,
    And wondered who before him would bear light
    With all the maidens in their rooms that night."

289

Telemachus then said: "this stranger here
Will bear my torch for he must earn his keep."
The nurse then left while he brought in the gear
To store while all the household was asleep.
Thus with his father he brought in the shields
And swords, and spears, and helms to hide away.
Athene with her golden lamp which yields
A light more beauteous that the dawning day,
Then went before them, but could not be seen.
Telemachus spoke of that wondrous light;
Odysseus said: "Be silent! It would seem
Some god has come to aid our task tonight."
    He said: "now take your rest yet I will stay
    To question all the maids, for soon comes day."

290

Penelope then from her chamber came,
Like Artemis or Aphrodite, gold,
And there she sat before the fire's warm flame
In a fine chair which craftsmen made of old,
Inlaid with ivory and silver curls
And with it a soft footstool for her feet;
Then, into the hall her white armed girls,
Came to clear the wine dregs and dry meat.
Replenishing the brazier with wood
They threw the dying embers on the floor,
Melanthe went where great Odysseus stood
And scolding him would drive him out the door.
 Odysseus asked the maiden, angrily,
 If she assailed him for his poverty.

291

He said that once he'd ruled a great estate
And freely gave when strangers came to him,
Yet by Zeus' will he'd lost all, now his fate
Was as she saw: a beggar wandering!
He warned Melanthe: "She might beauty lose!
Or cause the anger of the waiting queen,
Or if the king came home, for her abuse,
She would receive his retribution, keen."
Penelope then said: "Now shameless bitch
Your bad conduct is not hid from me,
On your own head will fall that vengeance which
Will wipe the stain from you, mercilessly.
 From my own lips you heard the strict command
 That I would meet this stranger to our land."

292

She said to Eurynome: "Bring a chair
And let the stranger sit and tell his tale,
About my husband, I am in despair,
Thus would ask him, which lands saw his sail?
And seek for news of one who long has gone.
First she asked him of his city state
And parentage, but the resourceful one
Deflected her with flattery and spake
Of how home thoughts would fill his heart with pain,
And bring disgrace if tears down his cheeks ran;
"All my beauty", said the noble dame,
"Went when my husband sailed for Ilion;
 I live with sorrows which some god brought down,
 Vile suitors woo me, wasting what we own.

293

I long for great Odysseus to return,
Avoiding all, I waste my heart away,
The suitors vie with gifts, my hand to earn,
Though I have tried all means to bring delay.
At first I told them I must weave a robe:
A shroud for great Laertes when death came,
To take him, and for three long years I strove,
By day I wove; at night by flickering flame
Unpicking what I'd done and by this ruse
Avoiding marriage, then in the fourth year
They came upon me, ending my excuse;
Now marriage, which I dread, comes ever near.
 My shameless maids had told the suitors all,
 Thus soon another prince will rule this hall."

294

The queen once more asked of his lineage,
And once again he spoke of his distress
Yet told her in Crete lay his parentage
In subtle tales so that she would not guess
That here, before her eyes, he had returned.
His well wrought story caused her tears to flow
Thinking of the one for whom she yearned,
Their streams flowed down her face like melting snow,
Which comes when eastern winds kiss mountain peaks.
Her lovely face dissolved in mourning's woe
As rivulets of anguish cleansed her cheeks;
Yet him sat with her, dare not sorrow show.
    He held his own tears back with eyes like steel,
    His purpose there he could not yet reveal.

295

When of weeping she had had her fill
She asked him of the clothes Odysseus wore;
The wily one said he remembered ill,
Long years had passed since then, a full two score.
He said: "A purple cloak comes to my mind,
The broach upon it gold, with double clasps,
With hound and dappled fawn it was designed,
One writhes to flee while tight the other grasps.
The tunic round his form was sheer and soft,
The sheen upon it glistened like the sun;
That garment may have been to him a gift
Or perhaps was his before his voyage began.
    A sword of bronze and cloak I gave to him
    Before he left once more to seek his kin.

296

A herald, Eurybates was his name,
Was honoured by that lord above the rest."
Then to the queen, sure recognition came
Of things her lord had with him when he left
Those shores for curséd Troy and that long war.
With tears she made reply: "that these were gifts
For one that she would welcome nevermore,
For with the dead his doleful spirit drifts."
Odysseus told her: "But you have my word!
Now cease your weeping for your lord is near,
Lately, in Threspotian lands I've heard
He'd been a guest, thus shortly must appear
 In Ithaca, here bringing riches vast
 To right your wrongs, and claim his throne at last.

297

From Thrinacea's king I've heard this tale:
He poured libations, then swore in his hall
That with your lord a ship was soon to sail.
I set out before him, sent to call
In Dulchium, the land of golden wheat;
Before I left he showed me that great wealth
Gained by your lord, and left at that king's seat;
For he had gone to learn if perhaps by stealth
He should return—from that high crested oak
In Dodona, where through rustling leaves,
In oracle, the voice of lord Zeus spoke
To those who sought to find what dark fate weaves.
 He swore, Odysseus would be there soon,
 Before the waxing of the coming moon.

298

Penelope then said: "Oh how I wish
That your promise to me is fulfilled!
To bring an end to years of my anguish,
That these things might occur, by great Zeus willed.
Then you would know the kindness of my heart,
And from my store be loaded down with gold,
Yet still I fear that he may not depart
And never reach his waiting hall's threshold."
She told her maidens: "Wash the stranger's feet
And then prepare for him a welcome bed,
Then when dawn comes you may your task complete
By bathing, then anointing, this poor head.
    Thus he may sit and dine at my son's side
    As our guest dressed fittingly, with pride."

299

Penelope decreed: "That who now dared
To vex this man, with pain would feel her wrath,
And he would find that miserably he fared
Hereafter, if at her guest he might scoff."
Odysseus, with much purpose, then replied
To say: "my hardship has been long and great,
Soft beds and baths have so long been denied,
Their pleasures now I would not contemplate,
Unless within her household there was one,
Old, true hearted, who had suffered much
She alone could bathe my feet or none,
If among her maids she had one such."
    Penelope called forth her ancient nurse
    Eurycleia, weak, with old age cursed.

300

She said that: "this old woman is the one
Who nursed Odysseus when he was a child."
She called to Eurycleia: "Rise and come!
And bathe this stranger, with us domiciled.
For her master's feet were such as those,
The man stood there was similar in age,
The old nurse then let loose hot tearful flows
And no word could her grief filled sobs assuage.
She wept about her long lost master's fate,
Then turning to the stranger said: "he too
Had suffered insult at this hall's great gate,
Thus she would tend him now as was his due."
    She murmured: "He resembles my lost lord,"
    Odysseus nodded, silent, in accord.

301

He said that often others had remarked
On his resemblance to the long lost king.
The nurse then took a cauldron down and worked
To fill it; much hot water she did bring.
When all was ready in that sheltered hearth
Odysseus then sat down, yet turned away,
Towards the dark, for in that welcome bath
His boar's tusk scar would, clear, be on display!
For this old wound the nurse knew very well,
And from it she would recognise her lord,
This might then unguarded words compel
And these would put the suitors on their guard.
    She washed his thigh, her hands began to shake,
    For she could not that ancient scar mistake.

302

A boar in old Parnassus made that wound
When he had gone to see Autolycus,
His mother's father, who by oath was bound
To give fine gifts to young Odysseus.
For he had said: "So let this child be named!"
When long ago he visited their land.
The old king said: "Let these great gifts be claimed
When he becomes a man, from my own hand.
His mother's mother: Ampithea, took
Him in her arms and kissed his head and eyes,
Whilst all around them gladly undertook
Their tasks, to ready bulls for sacrifice.
    Then all day long they sat, with joy, to feast,
    Till sunset came and brought the gift of sleep.

303

As soon as Dawn appeared they went to hunt,
With dogs, the sons of lord Autolycus;
Odysseus led them well out at the front
As they climbed the mount called Parnassus.
Through wild forest slopes at first they went
Till reaching windy hollows where boars roamed,
Before them went the dogs, keen on the scent,
Then all the young men with their spears well honed.
Nearby lay a boar in his thick lair
Well covered from the sun's hot rays, or rain,
Before those youths with spears could well prepare,
With bristling back and burning eyes he came!
    And for a moment stood there with no fear,
    While young Odysseus raised his hunting spear.

304

The boar was faster though and as he rushed
The wild beast charged, and just above the knee
His flesh was torn back by those scything tusks
Which missed the bone; so standing sturdily,
Odysseus then let fly and killed the boar,
His sure aim through its shoulder drove that spear;
The beast fell in the dust and made a roar
Which saw the fierce life in him, disappear.
Autolycus' staunch sons bound up the wound,
And checked the black blood's flow by magic charm,
Then butchering the carcass gathered round
And bore it homeward, down past field and farm.
 When healed they sent him back to Ithaca,
 With gifts; yet marked forever by that scar.

305

Eurycleia saw it as she washed
His leg and felt it with her gentle hands.
She dropped that limb and in the bronze it crashed
And spilled the water near the hearth's hot brands.
Her pounding heart was filled with joy and grief!
With tear filled eyes her heart caught in her throat!
She touched his chin with wonder and relief!
Then to Odysseus, she with soft voice spoke.
She said: "dear child, you are my sovereign who
I did not know until I touched your flesh."
Then to the queen her eyes, to tell her, flew;
Her master seized her biding her: now hush!
 He said: If hasty words she would employ,
 Revealing him she may her lord destroy.

306

He said: "you once had nursed me on your breast,
And now through many sorrows I have come,
In this twentieth year of my long quest
Despite the gods, at last I've reached my home.
Since you have found me out, keep silent now,
For fear that someone else will learn I'm here;
For if the gods my purpose, here allow:
To kill the suitors, words will cost you dear."
Eurycleia swore that she was true
And promised then to name those maidens all
Who'd brought dishonour; to whom death was due,
And those who had stayed guiltless in his hall.
    Odysseus said there was no need to tell
    Who was guilty, he would mark them well.

307

The old nurse brought more water for his feet,
Then bathed them and anointed them with oil;
He warmed himself when her task was complete,
Sat near the hearth, all prying eyes to foil.
He covered up the scar with his old clothes.
Penelope then came to him and spoke
Of all her dreadful sorrows and those woes,
Which in the night, like waves around her broke
To leave her mourning, lying ill at ease,
Just like that daughter of Pandareus:
The nightingale, who sings amid spring's trees
And wails for her lost child, called Itylus,
    Who by mistake, when human, she had slain;
    Forever, thus her song shrills out in pain.

308

She said her head was stirred in endless doubt,
Whether she should take a suitors hand
Or stay forever patient, holding out
In hope her lord would come back to their land.
Then she asked if he would hear her dream,
That he might sift its meaning as a seer,
Of twenty geese who entered her demesne
To feed, and fill her heart with joyful cheer.
Then an eagle, from his rocky heights,
Descended and broke all their necks in turn;
That war-bird then resumed his airy flight
Whilst she and all her women turned to mourn.
    He then returned and with a mortal voice,
    Perched on a beam, enjoined them to rejoice.

309

He said: "the geese were suitors, and your lord
Will soon return to loose an ugly doom
Upon their heads, with terror and discord."
She said: "on waking, looking round the room
I saw my geese, which fed on yellow wheat."
Odysseus told her: "this must be fulfilled,
Soon those creatures face their last defeat;
This prophecy was by the great gods willed."
Penelope had doubts, for she well knew
That clouded dreams could pass through different gates!
If through the one of horn they must be true
If through the one of ivory, the fates
    Had made them so they could not ever be,
    This must be so, for so the gods decree.

310

The queen could not believe it might be true,
And felt a dawn of evil name come near;
She set a task which all those there must do
To gain her hand and prove they were sincere.
She said twelve axe heads she would set in line,
Whoever with her lord's bow shot a shaft
Through them, would then by gods divine,
Win her by his strength and archer's craft.
The stranger said: "No longer this delay,
I swear that soon Odysseus will return."
Penelope though feared that baleful day,
And from his words no comfort could discern.
    She then went to her chamber, sad, to weep
    And left him near the hearth where he could sleep.

Book 20

311

Odysseus spread an ox-hide on the ground
And many fleeces, then beneath his cloak,
Laid, unsleeping, heard the galling sound
Of laughter from the faithless women folk,
Who slept with suitors and his house betrayed.
He wondered in his mind if he should rush
And kill them all, but his hand caution stayed;
He bade his raging heart within him: hush!
He must endure this insult of their ways.
Through it he brooded, fretful, without sleep
On how to end the shameless suitor's days;
For how could one, so many man-lives reap?
    Athene then appeared to him and asked:
    What concerns his wakeful spirit tasked?

312

He spoke about his fears and she replied,
Upbraiding him that he should ever doubt;
She said his vengeance could not be denied
And she would guarantee the suitors rout.
The goddess then brought sleep down on his eyes
And then to fair Olympus she returned.
High above, Penelope, with sighs,
And weeping for her absent husband yearned;
Then to mighty Artemis she prayed
For death or storms to carry her away,
As Pandareus's daughters were conveyed,
By tempests, to where Oceanus lay.
    There at his mouth the goddesses bestowed
    Those attributes, which queens alone are owed.

313

Aphrodite gave them honeyed wine
And cheese and honey so they would grow tall,
Chaste Artemis gave stature then, divine;
Hera: beauty, wisdom—above all
Other women, they were given skill
In handicrafts, by fair Athene then.
Great Aphrodite seeking to fulfil
Their futures sought out mates for all of them,
She went to Zeus to ask that happy boon.
The spirits of the storm though bore them up,
To be the furies servants was their doom,
The fates decreed, this be their bitter cup.
  Penelope thus prayed for such a fate
  Instead of life, with one that she would hate.

314

She said she wept by day and dreamt by night,
Such evil dreams the gods sent in her sleep.
Bright dawn then came, and waking to her plight,
Odysseus heard her sadly moan and weep.
She said last night she dreamed that she had lain
With her young lord of twenty years ago;
Odysseus mused, she thought that once again
She knew him, and that knowledge eased her woe.
He gathered up his bedding, then he prayed
To father Zeus and asked him for a sign;
On great Olympus thunder's voice he made,
To say he heard those prayers, that one divine.
  From those awaking near him in the hall
  He asked that words of omen now should fall.

315

Then a woman, grinding at her mill,
For she was old and slowest at that task,
Spoke to Zeus and wished the suitors ill,
Asking that this day should be their last;
For she had laboured grinding them their meal,
Until worn out by work, becoming weak;
Odysseus heard that old one thus reveal
The omen which his prayer was sent to seek.
Whilst other maids then came to make the fire,
Telemachus, the godlike, rose from bed;
Then dressed, and armed, he sought out Eurycleia
To ask how well their guest had slept and fed.
    Well reassured he left with two swift hounds,
    To where the suitors gathered, in his grounds.

316

Eurycleia busied all the girls
And made them sweep the hall; then on the chairs
Throw coverlets of purple for those earls
Who came to feast and plot, like craven curs.
With sponges they wiped clean the mixing bowls,
The double cups and table they prepared,
She sent off twenty to the water holes,
Whilst all the rest to household tasks repaired;
While men split logs to feed the greedy fires
The maids returned with water from the spring
And then: to satisfy those guest desires,
Eumaeus brought three boars for their feasting.
    He saw Odysseus and there inquired
    If he was treated as his heart desired.

317

Odysseus, darkly, told him of their ways,
Desiring that the gods might make them pay
He said: "such outrage runs through all their days
Their actions all our honour-codes betray."
As they spoke Melanthius came near:
The goat herd, bringing she-goats for the feasts;
He saw them and with taunts began to jeer,
Saying soon, they'd be antagonists,
And threatened with his fists to drive him off
For causing trouble as he asked for food.
Odysseus though, in silence, let him scoff
But with dark looks of hate, unspeaking, stood.
    A third man Philoetius then came
    With goats, and heifer, into his domain.

318

His beasts he tied beneath the portico,
Then asked Eumaeus whence the stranger came,
Of his kin and land he sought to know
Yet said: "He stands like one of kingly name,
Despite his beggar's garb and lowly state,
He is prince-like in his inward form."
He mused: "On him the gods conspire with fate,
To bring down sorrows on the noble born."
He stretched out to Odysseus his hand
In greeting, and spoke words of welcome there,
And wished him happy fortune in this land
Which drowned in evil: causing great despair.
    He said his master, if he lived must be
    Attired in rags and live in misery.

319

"If he is dead, then heavy woe is me!
A stranger bade me drive his cattle here
To feast upon, then make conspiracy
Of how they best can seize my master's gear.
Long since I would have fled but still I pray
That he may yet return and lay them low."
Odysseus said: "You soon will see him slay
The suitors if you wish, you have my vow."
The herdsman answered: "Would great Zeus fulfil
This promise, for my hands would give him aid."
Eumaeus joined in wishing those lords ill,
And to the gods for vengeance he then prayed;
    He prayed: the king be brought back to his hall,
    To mete out death and terror to them all.

320

The suitors meanwhile plotted death and doom
For his heir, when, swift, an omen came,
An eagle with a dove flew through the gloom
Then clutching that small bird flew off again.
Amphinomous advised them that their plan
Must go awry, thus they should drink and feast,
Those words from him there pleased every man;
Thus they laid their cloaks on chairs and seats
And fell to slaying all the goats and swine,
And that finest heifer, from its herd.
They roasted all the entrails then mixed wine,
With fresh bread brought the feast was well prepared.
    The suitors all sat down with that good cheer,
    To eat and drink, not knowing death was near.

321

Telemachus then made Odysseus sit
Near to the threshold on a shabby seat,
And gave him wine and food as was well fit
For any lord to drink, and gladly eat.
He said that any blow or insult thrown
He would deal with, as this was his home;
He told the suitors he would not condone
Ignoble deeds, he would such acts disown.
They bit their lips that he dare speak so bold,
Antinous, though told them to accept:
"For now his words the mighty gods allowed,
Now sit and feast, and cause him no regret."
    Then in Apollo's grove the feast began,
    With roasted portions set for every man.

322

Odysseus then, by his own son's command
Received the same as any lord sat there,
In Ctesippus the flames of anger fanned,
That he enjoyed such fine and ample fare.
Thus in sour tones he promised him a gift
And took an ox hoof, up from where it lay
And aimed it hard, and hoped that it would hit
The stranger, causing hurt, and much dismay.
Odysseus turned his head, the missile missed,
Yet in his heart he smiled a bitter smile;
Telemachus, who that foul deed witnessed,
Rebuked that lord, that he had dared defile
    The sacred hospitality, which there
    Protected all who that great feast should share.

323

He said that if the stranger had been struck,
Ctesippus, in turn, he would have speared,
He warned the others he would have no truck
With those who at the beggar, jibed and jeered.
He warned them all: If new dishonour came,
In violent combat he would rather die,
Than endure further insult to his name.
The son of Damastor then made reply:
That those words to him were justly said,
That they should show respect to guest or slave.
He said: "Sure now Odysseus must be dead
And in some far off land must lie his grave,
　　His wife should now thus choose the best of them,
　　And thoughts of marriage nevermore condemn."

324

Telemachus then, wisely, made reply
To Agelaus, swearing by great Zeus,
That he could not that marriage long deny,
For lost or dead must be Odysseus.
He said that she should take which man she would
And he would offer countless gifts beside,
Yet by compulsion though, he never could
Drive her from those halls to be a bride.
Athene addled all the suitor's wits
And drove wild laughter out, which seemed not theirs,
It issued forth from madly babbling lips,
Yet as they howled their eyes were filled with tears.
　　The very meat they ate seemed drenched with blood
　　And in their minds they mourned and saw no good.

325

The godlike Theoclymenus then spoke
To ask them what this evil was they saw?
He said: "Night shrouds you all like some dark cloak,
The very walls seem smeared with blood and gore.
The porch is full of ghosts and from the court
They hasten down to Erebus below."
But all the suitors laughed and made great sport,
They did not see that evil death-shadow.
Eurymachus, then called that good lord mad
And bade the heralds take him from that place;
He asked for guides, an escort he forbade,
He told them: soon would end their vile disgrace.
    He foresaw slaughter soon which none may cheat,
    The suitors all would deathless Charon meet.

326

He left those stately halls and came upon—
Piraeus, who gladly welcomed him.
Back in the hall the suitors tried the son
By mocking all his guests, but this sly whim,
For now, drew no response from that young lord,
Who watched his father, waiting for the time
When he would loose revenge on that foul horde,
Who now in turn threw insults and drank wine.
They called Odysseus: filthy vagabond!
Advising he be sold in Sicily.
Penelope, in silence, looked around
And watched as each man spoke, in misery.
    With glee they feasted laughing as they gorged,
    Not knowing of death's barbs, which fate had forged.

Book 21

327

Athene put a thought into the mind
Of wise Penelope, to bring the bow,
To set before the suitors who would find
A contest, which would let death enter now.
Up to her chamber then she took the key,
Then climbed the stairs into the furthest store,
She turned its handle made of ivory
And then threw wide the treasure house's door.
Amid the gold and bronze, in splendour lay
His back-bent bow and quiver of arrows:
A gift which mighty Iphilus one day
In Sparta gave him, marking friendship's vows.
    There, in their youth the two of them had met,
    When great Odysseus went, to claim a debt.

328

That fabled gift was given by a friend
Who afterwards was slain by Heracles,
Then when war demanded he attend
He would not take that bow across the seas,
But left it in his hall in memory
Of sacred friendship to a staunch comrade.
High above, its bow-case she could see
Where all the chests of fragrant clothes were laid.
Penelope sat down and took the bow
Out from its cover; seeing it she wept.
She thought then of her husband long ago
And their farewells, as he those shores had left.
    When she had done with weeping, down she went
    To where the suitors waited, ill content.

329

That quiver full of arrows they would find
Was full of groanings, which they all would taste!
Penelope, with handmaids stood behind,
Then spoke among those suitors who'd disgraced
Her home, and set a challenge for them all:
She said the first to string her husbands bow
And shoot a well aimed arrow down the hall,
Through twelve axe heads: with him she must then go!
As wife, forsaking all her memories
Of wealth and wedded life within that place.
The noble swineherd hearing her decrees
Set forth the bow, with prizes in that space,
    Abundances of iron and bronze to win
    And that fair lady, if they would begin.

330

When he saw the bow the cowherd wept,
And staunch Eumaeus let the hot tears flow,
Antinous rebuked them that they'd kept
Such sorrows in their minds from long ago.
He said their weeping pained the troubled queen
Whose heart still ached for her dear husband, lost;
He told them: "Weep where you cannot be seen,
Or sit in silence feasting with your host.
Yet leave that polished bow for all to try,
For they will find its curved wood hard to string,
For none here have the strength, not even I,
Which was possessed by Ithaca's great king.
    Yet in his heart he hoped he would succeed
    And from that place the prize, long hoped for, lead.

331

Telemachus set out the axes then,
In line, and challenged all to try the feat;
But said that he would, first, among those men
Try his father's bow, all to defeat;
For if he won his mother then must stay
And thus all suitors forfeit any claim.
Three times he strained, stood in the stone doorway,
To string the bow, that he the prize might gain,
And on the fourth he would have strung the bow
But stern Odysseus nodded, in dissent,
To tell his son he could not there allow
Success, and leave the suitors ill-content.
    The mighty youth thus laid the bow aside
    Disparaging that failure, in his pride.

332

He urged the suitors on to try their strength
And leant the bow against the polished door;
He then sat down to watch them; where at length
Each would take his place upon the floor.
Eupeithes great heir, then urged them on
To take that mighty challenge, each in turn.
The first arose, Leiodes; he was Oenop's son.
He seized the bow and shaft to try to earn
A noble wife, but soon his hands grew tired,
He laid the bow aside, for their dark seer
Had prophesied: to gain that thing desired,
Would cost those haughty princes very dear!
    He said it better then to die than live,
    For failure's stain could not proud hearts forgive.

333

Antinous rebuked him for those words,
In anger, saying: "if the bow can steal
The lives and spirits from those noble lords
Because he failed, their scorn he now must feel,
For this was due to weakness, his alone!
He said that one amongst them soon would string
That bow, and for his failure thus atone.
He called out to Melanthius to bring
A cake of fat, and stir up well the fire
So they could warm the bow and wax it smooth,
To make it supple as a well strung lyre,
Yet still they failed in turn each noble youth
 To string the bow, though none there wanted strength,
 Till midst them all just two were left at length.

334

Antinous remained then full of pride
And with him, for those left there were the best,
Eurymachus, the godlike, was untried.
Then the cowherd and the swineherd left,
Together, from the hall soon followed by
Odysseus, who stood outside by the gates
And spoke to both, in order each to try,
To find if they were true to his estates.
He asked them: "If your master now returned
Would you then defend him with your lives?"
They said: "That, 'by the gods' for this we've yearned,
That if nearby our noble king still thrives,
 For support our master will not lack,
 If only some kind god would guide him back!"

335

Odysseus then made answer to that pair,
For now, with certainty, he knew their hearts.
Explaining: "they no longer need despair
For with him now they both may play their parts
As here before them, was their king, returned!
For twenty years he'd fought through grievous toils
And they, alone, his gratitude had earned,
Both praying he'd survived those great turmoils,
Alone among the servants of his house."
He said that if some god would give him strength
To slay the suitors, while they all had cause,
He would make them rich men both, at length,
    With wives and houses they would be his friends
    If the suitors now got their just ends.

336

Then, as proof, he showed them that old wound
With which the boar had marked him long ago,
Now they knew their master they had found,
Both wept with joy to see that lost hero.
Odysseus checked their tears and told them: "cease
Your wailing, lest together here we're found,
Some suitor then may news of this release,
Which for a time by silence must be bound."
He told them they should follow him inside,
At different times, as though they had not met.
"Within, the bow to me will be denied,
For none among them can its string reset,
    If I should do it, I will bring down shame
    On all those gathered there of noble name.

337

Yet, you Eumaeus, as you bear the bow
Through the palace, place it in my hands;
Then tell the women: 'bar the great doors now!'
Be sure they all obey your dire commands,
And if they hear great groanings or loud din,
Command they sit in silence at their toils.
The courtyard gate must seal all captives in
Whilst death, inside, that lordly crowd embroils."
To Philoetius there he gave that task:
To bar the gate and fasten it with cord;
With all plans set he went inside at last
And took his seat amid their loud discord;
    For none of them could string the mighty bow;
    Eurymachus took the weapon now.

338

He warmed the wood and tried, and also failed,
Inside his heart he groaned then at the shame;
In anger then at all of them he railed,
None had the strength that sought for prize to claim.
None, to great Odysseus came near!
He mourned, no rival had such prowess there.
In times to come no doubt all men would hear
How none could match Laertes' noble heir.
Antinous though said they'd failed because
Upon this day there fell a godly feast,
And they must all obey the holy laws,
And for Apollo, each prepare a feast.
    Thus in the morning let the goat herd bring
    Prime she-goats here, to choose as offering.

339

From sacrifice to them would come: success!
Then, one would bend the bow to take the bride,
He called for wine there which the gods might bless,
And poured libation, not to be denied.
His words were pleasing, thus the wine was poured
First in libation, then in copious draughts
Into their cups, till satisfied each lord
Sat content and left the bow and shafts.
But then with cunning words Odysseus spoke
To say, as they had set aside the bow,
He prayed his words no anger would provoke,
If he took up the stave and tried it now;
    He merely sought that test to give them proof
    Of that great strength he'd had when in his youth.

340

Foul anger rose amongst them in their fear
That he might string the bow when they could not.
Antinous rebuked him making clear
That such as he could never try that shot,
And asked him if rich wine brought foolish words
Forth from his mouth? He told him: "be content
That you alone among the low swineherds
Sit with us feasting now, with our assent."
Reminding him of poor Eurytion:
That Centaur seized by madness, caused by wine;
He spoke about that drunken evil done
And punishment reaped from it, most condign.
    For with the bronze men sliced his ears and nose,
    Then cast him out, to show the world his woes.

341

He told him: "grievous harm will fall on you,
From all those here, if you can string the bow.
Then we will send you off to take what's due
From King Echetus, he lays all men low."
He said: "be still, and drink your wine in peace,
And do not try to strive with younger men."
Penelope spoke up then at that feast
To say, they robbed her guest of his due then,
Despite his station, he deserved his turn.
Asking, if he strung it did they think
He would hope a regal bride to earn,
And to his hovel with her, homeward slink?
    Eurymachus said: "They would all feel shame
    If some base fellow beat them at that game.

342

Then gossip would dishonour all those there
When it was heard: a beggar strung the bow!"
Penelope replied that none would care,
"For all your reputations are held low,
For you dishonour now a noble king."
She went on: "let the stranger take his turn,
To see if that great weapon he can string,
If he succeeds from me this man will earn
A cloak and tunic and a two edged sword,
A javelin to ward off dogs and men,
And sandals that his feet may stride abroad
To go wherever they might take him then."
    Telemachus then said: "no one but I
    May give the bow, or this great trial deny!"

343

He said: "In Ithaca, is my right
Alone among you all to give the bow."
He bade his mother to take out of sight
Her maidens, to their room and weaving, now.
She was seized by wonder at his speech
And swift obeyed and went upstairs and wept
For her noble husband, out of reach,
By aching years from her soft arms long kept.
The stalwart swineherd reached the weapon then
And picked it up, but all the lords cried out
And railed against him in that jealous den
That he should dare their haughty wishes, flout.
    Weighed down by threats from those of great renown
    He paused in fear, and put the weapon down.

344

Telemachus said: "father, carry on,
Pay no heed to them but obey me,
Complete your task and see that all is done
Or I will drive you off, to misery."
He wished out loud for strength much greater then,
So he could drive a few from his great hall,
In manner that they could not come again,
For wickedness they'd brought among them all.
This caused the suitors all to laugh with glee,
And thus the swineherd went on with the bow
To where the beggar sat where all could see:
His lord Odysseus, sat with knitted brow.
    He put the smooth wood in his master's hands,
    Then to the old nurse gave his stern commands.

345

He said that she must bar the hall's great door,
Whilst the stout cowherd sealed the courtyard gate,
He took up woven rush rope from the floor
And wound it round, so none could then escape.
He next came in and sat and watched his lord
Who held and turned the bow like some old friend.
The suitors watched, concerned, then in accord
Agreed a master's hand must that wood bend.
They tried that sight, with words, to put aside,
For fear that beggar might outdo their strength,
But he had now, the stave, on all sides tried,
He lifted up that well made bow at length
 And strung it then as one who plays the lyre,
 With ease, with twisted sheep-gut, near the fire.

346

He took it in his right hand, tried the string,
Which like a swallow sang beneath his touch,
The suitor's faces paled with sorrowing,
That this low one had there achieved so much.
Great Zeus above them thundered forth his signs!
Odysseus heard that omen come with joy;
He knew the gods approved his dark designs,
Which soon those wastrel suitors would destroy.
He thus took up an arrow, lying bare
Upon the table—notched it on the string—
Then drew it back and sitting in his chair
Loosed the shaft, with certain aim, to sing
 Through all twelve axe-head holes, he could not miss,
 His skill would bring those vile lords: nemesis.

347

He then addressed Telemachus, to say:
"The stranger sat here brings no shame on you,
I sent the bronze tipped arrow on its way
And did not miss as all saw, in full view;
Nor did I labour as I strung the bow,
That strength I had in youth is with me yet!
I rose above the suitors taunts to show,
That they might soon their evil words regret."
He said though: "now is time for wine and song,
For feasting while we still enjoy the light,
Thus bring the lyre, and play those tunes divine,
That we may greet, in merriment, this night."
 His son armed with the gleaming bronze drew near
 And at his father's side stood, with his spear.

Book 22

348

Odysseus stripped his rags—the sign was made,
He sprang, armed with the bow into the hall,
The quiver, emptied, at his feet was laid,
Its contents, spilled out, ready for them all.
He said: "the contest, clearly, now is won!"
Then he sought to hit another mark,
He prayed Apollo granted this be done
And picked an arrow ready for the work.
Antinous was target for that shaft
As he raised up the two eared golden cup,
The wine which touched his lips would be his last,
The arrow pierced his throat and blood flew up,
 Out through his nostrils as he kicked and writhed
 Then mid the food spilled on the floor, he died.

349

The suitors sprang, in uproar, from their seats,
Spurred by fear throughout that lofty hall,
For there Laertes' son dark vengeance seeks.
They looked for shields or spears upon each wall
But these were hidden well, and locked away;
Thus they with cursing words attacked him now,
Odysseus though, then brought them great dismay,
With hate filled words and dark and angry brow.
He said: "you dogs! You never thought that I
Would ever come back from the Trojan wars,
You waste my house and with my maids you lie
And try to take my wife, like craven curs;
 Insulting all the laws of gods and men,
 You thought you were exempt from all of them.

350

He said: "Destruction's cords now bind your feet!"
Then pallid fear seized hold of all of them.
Darting eyes saw only their defeat
And no escape routes from that deathly den.
Eurymachus, alone there made reply,
And tried to blame the lord Antinous,
For setting on those deeds, so all would try
To win the lands of great Odysseus.
He promised recompense for what was done
And twenty oxen's worth of bronze and gold,
To assuage his hate, from everyone;
He said: "The one who caused this all, lies cold."
    With angry words Odysseus answered him
    For evil they would pay, in life and limb.

351

Thus all their knees were loosened where they stood,
With melting hearts they looked on him in fear;
Eurymachus, thus urged they take his blood
And urged them: draw their swords and then get near
That hero using tables as their shields,
Against those deadly arrows which brought death,
"For that must surely come to him who yields,"
Now they must fight or sink beneath the earth.
He forwards sprang and drew his two edged sword,
At that same time Odysseus let fly,
And struck him with the shaft and that vile lord,
Pierced through the liver, screaming, fell to die.
    He writhed and with his brow beat on the floor,
    Till Thanatos away his spirit bore.

352

Amphinomus then rushed upon the king,
Telemachus though stuck him from behind,
With mighty strength he let the bronze spear wing:
All saw its point through bone and muscle grind.
The lance drove through his chest and down he fell,
His forehead struck the ground with awful sound:
The father stood with arrows to repel
Those others whilst his son their armour found,
And shields and spears for all, the herdsmen too,
With helmets for those four that they might fight
And ward off all those deadly blows which flew
From suitors, desperate now with deathly fright.
    He armoured first himself and then his slaves
    So all might stand and fill those wastrel's graves.

353

While he had arrows still Odysseus aimed
And killed those curs, who now fell thick and fast;
But when his stockpile failed the bow he leaned
Against the door and armed himself at last.
With four fold shield and well wrought helm he stood,
Its horsehair plume waved death threats from on high;
With two stout spears he sought to draw more blood
And with the bronze invite them all to die.
Above, set in the wall, a postern gate
Led out into a narrow passage way,
Odysseus sent the swineherd there to wait
And hold the suitors, if they fled, at bay.
    The way was narrow and one valiant man
    Could bar that path, which to the outside ran.

354

Agelaus enquired about the gate,
Melanthius though said the route was barred,
Yet offered from the storeroom arms to take
And bring them, to equip each fretful lord.
He went above and brought twelve shields and spears
And helms with armour for them to put on;
Odysseus told his son then of his fears
That to the store some miscreant had won.
They saw the goatherd go for armour bright,
And sent Eumaeus, swift, to close the door,
With the cowherd, there they seized that wight
And bound him tight, hung high above the floor.
    They sealed the door and left him, hung, in pain,
    While they went down to join the fight again.

355

The four stood steadfast, fury in their breath,
But still faced many; now well armed and brave.
Athene came into that hall of death
In Mentor's form, and to Odysseus gave
Such hope! He asked his friend to join with them
To help them ward off ruin in that fight;
Agelaus upbraided Mentor then,
That he should help those four in their sore plight.
He said that: "When the suitors kill them all
He would share their fate and lose his lands,
And dire fates to your women will soon fall
As they suffer at their vengeful hands."
    Athene though grew angry at those words
    And in those hero's hearts new courage stirred.

356

Reminding him of all those years in Troy,
And how his courage in those ranks held sway;
She urged him in his own house to employ
That valour, which in past years, won the day.
Then as a swallow to the roof she flew,
And high above perched mid the smoky beams;
Agelaus then urged them to renew
Their efforts and attack in separate teams.
Six at first he called, the best of those
Of all the suitors who, alive, remained,
Damastar and Peisander arose,
Ampimedon and Polybus, well famed.
    With them stood lord Demoptolemus,
    Last, beside him rose Eurynomus.

357

With all the arrows gone he told them throw
Their spears, hoping Odysseus to hit,
They hurled them dreaming Zeus might then bestow
High glory on them all but none of it
Would fall on them, for seated high above
Athene's spells ensured those missiles missed.
Odysseus told his comrades they must prove
Their prowess thus returning lances hissed
Through vacant air, and each one hit its mark,
Demoptolemus and Euryades fell
Peisander, also went into the dark:
All three at the same time thus entered hell.
    But other suitors stepped up to retrieve
    Those spears, in hope their targets to achieve.

358

Again they hurled their lances eagerly,
Athene saw that most were thrown in vain
Telemachus was struck, all cried with glee,
But looked on his grazed hand with low distain.
Ctessipus' long spear, Eumaeus touched
Yet passed above his shoulder with no harm,
But then Odysseus and his fellows launched
Their deadly spears, with venom, overarm.
Telemachus hit lord Amphimedon,
Odysseus brought Eurydamus down,
The life of Polybus the swineherd won,
Through Ctessipus the cowherds lance had flown.
    He said that: "For the hoof you've lately thrown
    This is my gift, returned to you alone."

359

Odysseus wounded haughty Agelaus
With a deadly thrust of his long spear,
Telemachus brought down Leocritus,
His point drove through the groin and came out clear,
He fell down head-long, dead, he struck the ground;
And then Athene held the Aegis up
Which caused the suitors all to run around
Like cattle bit by gadflies, panic-struck.
As doves, with no escape, when vultures swoop
To scour the plain and rend them with their claws,
The suitors flew, demented, round their coup
In search of open windows or wide doors.
    The four advanced then striking right and left,
    The floor swam red with blood from head and chest.

360

Leiocles then rushed out and clasped the knees
Of Odysseus, and with wingéd words
Beseeched his mercy there, with humble pleas,
Amid the groans of those vile dying lairds.
He swore that he had tried to check them all
And had no woman wronged by word or deed.
The great lord scowled above him in that hall
And said: "Your prayers are drenched in vice and greed,
As their soothsayer, with them you must die!"
Then with his hand he seized a nearby sword
And sliced his neck through leaving him to die:
He fell to earth while speaking his last word.
  Then Phemius the minstrel also came
  To kneel before the king with mercy's claim.

361

He put aside his lyre and grasped the knees
Of lord Odysseus, and asked for grace,
He said the suitors forced him to their sprees,
By harsh compulsion, there he took his place.
He said: "Your son will vouch that this is true,
That I with great reluctance came to sing;"
Telemachus replied, This well he knew,
"This man is guiltless!" To the vengeful king.
As was the herald Medon, wise of heart,
Who heard him, huddled safe beneath a chair,
Under an ox-hide skin he'd hid to thwart:
That deadly fate, which claimed all others there.
  He rose in fear and made a sacred oath,
  That in all deeds done there he'd honoured both.

362

Odysseus smiled and said that he was saved,
And with the minstrel now should wait outside
While he made sure those princes, vile, depraved,
No longer hid in fear; that all had died.
The two went out and by the altar sat
And looked always around, expecting death,
The king searched through the hall, ensuring that
No suitors there remained who drew sweet breath,
But all lay silent in the blood and dust,
Like fish spilled out from nets drawn from the sea;
All lay heaped in payment for that lust
Which brought them there, to woo Penelope.
    Odysseus told his son to call the nurse,
    So he might new commands to her disburse.

363

She came down to that hall of blood and looked
And saw her master fouled, with dirt and gore,
And how death's god those tainted souls had plucked,
To wander now in Hades evermore.
Her lord then like a lion who had fed
Fresh on a farm ox, stood and gave command
That now those wanton servants he must lead
Down to the hall, that they might understand
Their shame and what dark fate awaited them,
Eurycleia to him made reply,
Twelve, of fifty, lay with those vile men,
And for their shamelessness they now must die.
    With joy filled heart at what had there been done
    The old nurse went, to bid those wantons come!

364

Odysseus told his son and herdsmen then:
"Now move the bodies, wipe away the blood
And with sponges cleanse this gory den,
Let these women help you make all good.
Then lead them to the courtyard and with swords
End all thoughts of Aphrodite's joys.
The women came then, wailing at his words,
And cleaned the hall, then led by death's envoys
Were taken to the courtyard and all hanged.
Telemachus would not allow swift death,
Remembering how he had been harangued
By those who kicked the air and gasped for breath,
    With nooses round their necks he pulled them high
    On a ships cable, so they all might die.

365

They then led out Melanthius and sliced
His nose and ears and hands off with their blades,
Tore out his private parts and sacrificed
Them raw, for dogs to eat for his tirades
And insults to his master, when he came.
Odysseus then asked the staunch old nurse,
To bring down sulphur to wipe out that stain
Of those who'd fouled his hall with death's dark curse.
He told her: "Tell Penelope to come
With all her maidens, for we now may meet."
A fire was made, and all he willed was done,
And then the nurse brought down those maidens, sweet.
    Embraces fell on him and in soft showers
    Their kisses healed his heart with love's great powers.

Book 23

366

The old nurse went upstairs and laughed aloud,
With joy, and told her mistress all the news:
How well-earned death had felled the suitors, proud,
And how those wanton maids had paid their dues.
The queen heard all her words in disbelief
And said: "the gods have led my mind astray,
To tell me this has ended years of grief
But woken now the sorrows of this day."
She told the nurse her age held back her rage,
Yet Eurycleia stood, insisting still
That he had come! He'd sent this ancient sage
To bring her now, it was her master's will!
 He was that ragged stranger she had seen,
 He waited now below to greet his queen.

367

Penelope was glad and swiftly rose
And then embraced the nurse, and shed warm tears,
She asked that, patient, old one to disclose
How the awful suitors gained their biers.
She said: "I heard the groaning of those men,
As they were killed; but did not see them fall.
With all the serving maids, in terror then,
We'd locked ourselves away from that dark hall
Until I heard your son call out for me,
I came and found Odysseus mid that gore;
The suitors all had met their destiny
Each lay, in red blood soaked, upon the floor.
 He stood there like a lion in that crowd
 Besmeared by gore, victorious and proud.

368

The bodies all are gathered at the gate,
With sulphur now the precinct is made clean,
A mighty fire lies kindled in the grate,
And he has sent me now to bring his queen.
For all that he desired has been restored:
He has his wife and son and fertile lands."
Penelope still doubted that her lord
Could now have slaughtered all those foul brigands.
She said: "sure some immortal in disguise,
Has killed them in full payment for their deeds,
Their wanton folly led to their demise;
The vengeance of the gods on evil feeds."
    That hope, which in her heart so long had slept,
    Disturbed her mind and this could not accept.

369

The nurse then told her of the boar tusk's scar
And said: "her life was forfeit if she lied!"
Penelope thus left her safe boudoir
To see if those foul lords had really died.
She went downstairs and saw what had been done,
Then sat and looked to where her husband stood.
She stared there, in amazement, looking long,
First, at his face then at his beggar's hood.
She could not there decide if it was he
But stayed in silence seated by the fire.
Telemachus rebuked her, cruelly,
That she held back her long pent up desire,
    To greet her husband after twenty years,
    The queen spoke up, to quiet all his fears.

370

She said that she would know him by and by,
By secret signs, known only by those two;
Odysseus smiled and said she would soon try
Him in those halls, and greet him when she knew
It was indeed her husband, there returned;
But he was dirty now and thus should bathe
Before she talked to him, as long she'd yearned;
The clothes he stood in made him look a slave.
Telemachus he told: "our deadly deeds
Could bring revenge, and we must have a care,
A single killing often vengeance breeds,
If he who dies is someone's son and heir.
    As many youths of noble blood they'd slain,
    This they must justify, with reasons plain.

371

Resourcefully, then lord Odysseus spoke,
Urging, they should bathe and don new clothes,
And then the minstrel's lyre should make all folk
Think some fine celebration there arose.
This stratagem should then delay the news
Of how the suitors died within those walls,
Then with Olympian help they may excuse
Their actions, and with help defend those halls.
Then all was done as their great lord had said,
With all prepared they heard the hollow lyre,
Resounding in that place where souls had fled;
Replacing shadowed death with sweet desire.
    Thus, those who roamed about and heard that sound
    Said: "Now a husband our fair queen has found."

372

They said that she was cruel to now give way
And wait no longer for her man's return;
They did not know, once more the king held sway
And all the suitors lay beyond concern.
Eurynome bathed her rightful lord,
Anointing him with oil, and then brought clothes,
A splendid cloak and tunic from her hoard,
And dressed him, as befitting, in those robes.
Athene shed great beauty round his form,
Increased his stature, and from his fine head
Made locks to flow in curls and thus transform
Him from a beggar to a king, high bred.
    He came and, godlike, sat down near his wife
    Then said: "Your heart is hard and full of strife

373

That after twenty years, you stand aloof
From your true lord, who now, his home has claimed."
She would not greet him there beneath that roof,
With heart like iron, she now her lord disdained.
He told the nurse that they must sleep apart
And bade her make a couch up for a bed;
Penelope searched deeply in her heart
For words to test him, she still lived in dread
That some cruel god her senses now deceived.
She told the nurse: "outside her chamber door,
Near her bedstead, there he would be received,
And she should make it in that place therefore
    And on that stout frame cloaks and fleeces stow,
    Then coverlets, above all that must throw.

374

She spoke those words, intending thus to test
Her noble husband, who grew angry then;
He asked: "why did she taunt her kingly guest
Who'd fixed that bed in place, inside his den,
He'd built it strong around an olive's trunk,
With close set stones, well roofed and with stout doors;
An adze into those branches he had sunk,
Then formed the frame with augers and sharp saws;
Ivory and silver, gold, he'd used,
As inlays, with a purple ox-hide thong,
He said: No man, with ease, my work has moved
Unless he'd wrecked that olive trunk, so strong."
 Penelope thus heard her husband speak,
 And at his words her trembling knees grew weak.

375

She recognised those proofs Odysseus showed:
That there indeed before his wife he stood!
She rushed to him and gave that love long owed,
With many kisses now, in certitude:
That here at last her long lost lord was home!
She asked forgiveness for that test she'd made
And said her heart was fearful, here alone,
That some vile stranger would her bed invade,
With guileful words seducing her for gain;
Her lord described that bed which they alone
And Actor's daughter knew, in her domain:
Then Odysseus wept for he was home!
 There at last he held his steadfast wife,
 Delivered thus from all his trials and strife.

376

On their weeping dawn might then have risen,
Had not Athene seen long night detained
By Oceanus, in his gloomy prison,
She held day's steeds lest they be yoked and reined
To draw Dawn's car across the waiting sky.
Odysseus though, then urged that they should rest;
Penelope his wish could not deny.
He told her trials still waited, both to test.
She asked of them and her great lord explained
How blind Tiresias had sent him on
With one curved oar, till on dry land detained,
And asked if there he bore winnowing fan?
    Then he fixed the curved oar in the earth
    With sacrifice to lift Poseidon's curse.

377

"I made him offerings then, and when safe home
Would lay great hecatombs before the gods,
Then gentle death, far from the sea's wild foam
Would take me, when at last sleek old age nods.
Penelope said: this gave her new hope
That threatened evils might be overcome!
Thus with joy that pair, contented, spoke
For they could rest at last in their kingdom.
The old nurse Eurynome made their bed
And came up to the bridal chamber door,
First, to the joys of love those two were led
And then wove tales, their lost years to explore.
    Penelope told how she had endured
    With hope alone, deep in her heart inured.

378

Odysseus then recounted all his woes
Of lotus-eaters, Circe, and the rest,
How he alone escaped from danger's throes,
And with Phaeacian aid came home at last.
Then sweet sleep came, and when Athene saw
That he had dreamed sufficiently she roused
Pale Dawn, who then across the sea light bore,
From night's dark tomb, where long it had been housed.
Odysseus woke, and left his wife to hold
His wealth and hall and went up to the farm
With his son, and both, and his herdsmen bold,
Well armed, prepared to deal with hurt and harm.
 He said news of the suitors must soon spread,
 Of where they lay, now lying bloodied, dead.

Book 24

379

They left the city, went to his estate,
To find his father: old Laertes, there;
Meanwhile, Hermes led down to their fate
The suitor's ghosts, who gibbered in despair.
He took them down dank ways, past Ocean's streams,
And Leuca's rock, and the gates of the sun
To that meadow, in the land of dreams,
Of Asphodel, where life and hope is done.
Forever there, pale ghosts and phantoms dwell;
They found Achilles bold, and Patroclus,
And Aias, who all heroes did excel
But for that peerless son of Peleus.
    They thronged around that chieftain, tall and proud,
    Till Agamemnon's ghost approached that crowd.

380

With him came those others of the dead
From the bloody halls of Aegisthus,
Achilles ghost addressed him first and said:
That you above all men were dear to Zeus,
Despite that, you too met an early doom,
Ignobly, it was better you had died
In Troy, then all could there have built your tomb."
Agamemnon, sadly, then replied:
"Godlike son of Peleus you fell
In glory, fighting near the walls of Troy,
Many joined you there in death as well
As Trojans tried to seize and then destroy
    Your noble corpse; we battled all day long,
    To save your body from that warlike throng.

381

We bore you to the ships and cleansed you well,
With ointments and warm water as you lay
Upon your bier, then tears of mourning fell
From those Danaans, thronging in dismay.
They cut locks from your hair, and when she heard
Your mother rose up from the sea-green deeps,
Immortal sea nymphs came and all despaired,
And fear and trembling seized those waiting Greeks.
All would have fled, but Nestor held them there
With words of wisdom, calming, and benign:
That Thetis rose up from her shady lair
To look on her son's face for one last time.
    Thus, flight then ceased and all Greeks stood to mourn
    With those daughters from the sea god born.

382

In immortal raiment you were clothed
And then the muses, nine, led off the dirge;
All who saw you there to death betrothed,
Let bitter tears their painful sorrow purge.
Seventeen days, by day and night, we mourned
And on the eighteenth gave you to the fire;
With many beasts your noble form was burned
And all, in armour, circled round your pyre.
Then when Hephaestus' flames an end had made
We gathered at the dawning your white bones;
In a gold urn with perfumes these we laid,
With unmixed wine and many mourning moans
    With those of noble Patroclus, your friend;
    We gave them to the great tomb to defend.

383

Built on a headland by the Hellespont
So that it might be seen far out to sea,
Thetis saw in death you would not want,
For then came funeral games, and victory
Gave prizes from the gods, which she had brought,
Set there in your honour, for your fame;
Then won by fabled kings who by their sport
Preserved forever, your immortal name.
Alas, for me great Zeus devised dark doom
Brought by Aegisthus, and my curséd wife.
Then, as they spoke came Hermes through the gloom
Leading those whom lately'd ended life.
    Amongst them, seen by Agamemnon's ghost,
    Was Amphimedon, who once had been his host.

384

The great king asked him by what means they'd come,
Beneath the dark earth, in the prime of youth?
Enquiring how cruel fate their lives had won,
In man made wars or through some god's reproof?
Amphimedon, then went through all the tale,
Of how they'd wooed Penelope, who strove
Through long days at her loom to no avail,
For during night, she that day's work, un-wove:
When her deceit was at long last revealed
She lay compelled to wed, with task complete.
Odysseus then returned, at first concealed,
And lead his band the suitors to defeat
    With arrows from his bow; stood with his son
    And herdsmen, they dealt death till all was done.

385

Above, his hall's floors drank up all our blood,
It was the will of Zeus that we must die;
Each man fell, no matter where he stood,
We perished there, unwashed our bodies lie,
Outside his hall, unknown to all our friends."
Agamemnon praised Penelope
And said: "Her name will live for she defends
Her vows and would be praised in poetry
Which would through time preserve her honoured name.
His own wife's deeds would win reviling words,
For hateful was her act and full of shame;
Which all would learn of, when they heard the bards."
    Thus, the two men spoke in Hades depths
    Of how they each had won, unwanted deaths.

386

Up above Odysseus and his men
Had left the town and found Laertes' farm,
Which lay, well ordered, in a vine rich glen
With restful ways amid soft meadowed calm.
His bondsmen lived there, and a servant, old,
Who tended him, inside, with kindly care.
Odysseus told his men to now take hold
Of his best swine, and then a feast prepare,
While he sought out his father mid those groves.
He went down to the vineyards then and found
His father working, wearing ox-hide gloves,
Alone there without slaves he tilled the ground.
    Odysseus saw him worn by grief and years,
    And standing near a pear tree, shed salt tears.

387

Odysseus debated in his mind
If he should go and greet his father there,
Or, if with testing words to try and find
What thoughts gripped that old man, in his despair.
The son addressed the father, mockingly,
And asked whose slave he was, who laboured, old
Tending orchard grounds, in misery,
In his last years by waiting death paroled.
He asked if this indeed was Ithaca
To which he had now come with all his men;
He said to find that isle he'd travelled far
To try to find a long lost friend again.
    He wondered if he lived here still, at ease,
    Or was dead, long gone down to Hades.

388

That friend had claimed to be Laertes' son,
And as such was richly entertained,
Was given much gold and mantles, richly spun,
And other gifts as their guest code ordained.
Laertes answered, weeping, that indeed
The stranger now to that home isle had come,
But told him: "wanton suitors filled with greed
Now hold those lands which, hard, my heir had won."
Enquiring then, how many years had passed
Since he had entertained that noble lord,
Whom evil fate had on some far shore cast,
Or swallowed in dark depths, lost overboard.
    He felt, undoubtedly, his son was dead,
    With none to mourn him, on his funeral bed.

389

He then approached that stranger there to ask:
Who he was and by what means he'd come?
Odysseus said: His home was Alybas,
And to the lord Apheides he was son.
He ran on with that tale with his false name
And said his guest had left five years ago.
About Laertes, clouds of grief then came,
And he took up dry dust and poured it slow
Upon his grizzled hair with many groans.
Odysseus' heart then felt a sharp grief pang
On hearing his old father's plaintive moans;
To comfort him, thus up at once he sprang
    And took him in his arms and straightway said:
    "I am your son, returned now from the dead!"

390

Odysseus then explained what he had done
And told his father: "Haste is needed now."
Laertes said: "if you are my dear son
Some sign, in proof, to me you must now show."
Odysseus, first, the boar's tusk scar revealed,
And then named all those trees which as a youth
His father gave him, set in grove and field.
Laertes saw that he had told the truth,
And flung his arms in welcome round his son;
Yet sank down, failing, weak with joy and grief,
But then thanked all the gods for what was done
For now, from years of woe he'd gained relief.
    He said he feared that for each suitor's life
    His clan would come, to try exact some price.

391

Resourcefully, Odysseus made reply,
And said that they must first go up to dine,
For now their meal must on the table lie
With meat all carved, next to the sparkling wine.
Young handmaidens from Sicily then bathed
Laertes and anointed him with oil;
Athene, next came down and round him swathed
A look of youth, which caused all to recoil
In wonder at how strong and tall he stood.
Odysseus said: "some god has made this so!"
Laertes wished as such he'd shed the blood
Of those vile suitors, laying many low.
  Then from the fields old Dolius came near,
  They told him, sit, and join in their good cheer.

392

Dolius then kissed Odysseus' hand
In greeting and inquired if he should send
Out to the queen a slave at his command,
So this news she now might comprehend.
Odysseus reassured him that she knew
That Dolius' sons approached their land to greet
Him in that manner, which to him was due,
He then told all to sit with him and eat.
As they feasted, rumour did its rounds:
That messenger which like wild fire, spreads news.
Thus people came from all the township's bounds,
Up to the suitor's final rendezvous;
  To take the corpses each to his own home,
  And gather later, leaving them, alone.

393

When they were assembled, Eupeithes
Arose in grief, to speak about his son:
Antinous, and there with tearful pleas:
Asked that they should seek revenge, as one!
He said Odysseus in his swift ships
Had led the best young men with him to war,
And none returned! "Now, see how fresh blood drips
From those hands which come, our heirs to mar.
The minstrel, Medon, came up from the hall
And said: "Those deaths were sanctioned by the gods,
One there I saw. Thus pale fear seized them all."
On hearing how men fell, against all odds.
    Old Halisthernes, weighing what was done
    Said: "through folly, was deservéd justice done!

394

Your sons, through wanton wickedness have died!
If we seek revenge we too might fall."
Some held back, but half for vengeance cried
For now the blood lust held them in its thrall.
Athene spoke to Zeus, great Cronos' son,
To ask if he would bring down evil war,
Or would he let the gift of peace be won
By one who'd suffered much and travelled far.
Zeus spoke, and said that she'd devised that plan
Resulting in the suitors sad demise;
That choice was hers but now these fresh thoughts ran
Within his mind: that peace should now arise!
    They all should swear an oath: that there for life
    Odysseus should be king, and end all strife.

395

He said the gods would bring the people peace
And let them all forget those bloody deeds.
He granted then the goddess her release:
From high Olympus, down, her pathway leads!
With feasting ended great Odysseus spoke,
Asking someone now to go and see
How near or far off were those vengeful folk
Who came in vain, with hopes of victory.
Old Dolius went out and saw them near,
Odysseus said his comrades all should arm;
Thus sons and elders donned their battle gear
And then went out to answer war's alarm.
    Athene, clothed as Mentor, then drew near
    And with words of brave deeds, aroused good cheer.

396

Athene told Laertes: "Make a prayer
To mighty Zeus, then raise and hurl your spear."
And then she furnished old Arceisus' heir
With mighty strength so he might persevere.
He threw that weapon, straight and swift it flew,
Piercing lord Eupeithes through his helm.
Telemachus, and his great father drew
Their swords and spears and ran to overwhelm
The rest stood there; they would have killed them all.
But flashing eyed Athene ordered: cease!
All stopped dead, in terror, at her call
And dropped their arms and fled in hope of peace,
    Towards the city, headlong, in retreat,
    Flying homewards, certain of defeat.

397

Pursuing them, Odysseus loudly roared
And swooped upon them like an eagle proud.
Zeus, with lightning, showed his strong accord
And spurred their flight, with sounds of thunder, loud.
Then, flashing eyed Athene gave command:
That now at last Laertes son should cease,
And end this strife of war, and stay his hand
As now from all his trials he'd gained release.
In his heart Odysseus was glad
For he had now come home, to rest at last.
    This tale I started with the Iliad
    Is now complete, and in these sonnets cast.

Glossary of Names

Where it is obvious who the person is, especially in respect of the minor characters; the name may not be included.

Achaea: A Greek Province. (Greece generally).

Aeaea: Island where Circe lived. It can be used as a name for Circe herself.

Aegisthus: Seducer of Clytemnestra who was the wife of Agamemnon. Together they murdered him on his return from Troy.

Aegyptus: According to Greek myth, founder of the kingdom of Egypt.

Aeolus: God who controlled the winds.

Agelaus: One of the suitors.

Aias: Telamonian Ajax. The great Greek warrior hero, second only to Achilles.

Aithiopes: Inhabitants of the far southern lands (Ethiopians).

Alcinous: King of the Phaeacians. Father of Nausicaa and husband of Arete.

Amphinomus: A suitor who was given the chance to leave by Odysseus, due to his civility; he chooses to stay and is the third of them to die.

Antinous: The vilest, and first to die of the suitors.

Antilochus: Nestor's eldest son.

Argeiphontes: An alternative name for Hermes as god of dawn.

Argives: An alternative name for the Greeks.

Ares: Greek god of war.

Arete: Wife of Alcinous.

Artemis: Daughter of Zeus by Leto. Twin sister of Apollo. On earth virgin goddess of childbirth, fertility and hunting. In the heavens called Selene and in the underworld Hecate.

Athene: Athena. Virgin goddess of agriculture, cities, war, wisdom and handicrafts. Mother of Apollo.

Atreides: The sons of Atreus, Agamemnon and Menelaus.

Autolycus: The father of Odysseus' mother, Anticleia. He is a famous thief and liar in the Greek myths.

Calypso: A sea goddess who lived on the isle of Ogygia. She saved Odysseus when his ship was wrecked on her island but then held him there for seven years as her lover until the gods ordered his release.

Castor: One of two twins, the Dioscuri — Castor and Polydeuces (in Latin: Pollux).

Chloris: Mother of Nestor.

Cicones: Allies of the Trojans who had settlements in Thrace.

Circe: A powerful sorceress who could turn humans into animals. She lived on the island of Aeaea.

Clytemnestra: Wife, and with her lover Aegisthus, joint murderer of Agamemnon.

Dardanians: Alternative name for the Trojans.

Demeter: Greek goddess of corn, and thus the sustainer of life.

Diomedes: One of the great heroes who fought on the Greek side at Troy.

Eidothea: Daughter of the sea god Proteus.

Epicasta: Name used in Homer for Jocasta.

Eurylochus: One of the comrades and brother-in-law of Odysseus.

Eurymachus: Second of the suitors to be killed.

Eurytion: A Centaur.

Furies: The Greek goddesses of retribution; also known as the Erinyes or Eumenides.

Hades: The underworld. The term can also apply to Hades the king of the underworld.

Halitherses: A wise seer.

Harpies: Winged goddesses of the storm winds who suddenly snatch people up so they are never seen again.

Helen: The great beauty Helen of Troy.

Helios: Term used to describe the sun god and the sun itself.

Hephaestus: The Greek god of metalworking and fire.

Hyperion: Another name for the sun god, also the name of one of the Titans.

Iasion: Son of Zeus and Electra.

Icarus: Father of Penelope.

Idomeneus: King of Crete.

Ilus: Founder of Ilium, otherwise known as Troy, after his father Tros.

Ino: A sea goddess.

Ithaca: The home island of Odysseus.

Itylus: The nightingale; otherwise known as Aedon.

Lacedaemon: A son of Zeus who married the Laconian princess, Sparta. The country was named after him and its capital after his wife.

Laertes: The aged father of Odysseus.

Laestrogonians: A race of man eating giants.

Leda: Wife of the Spartan king Tyndareos. Famed for being seduced by Zeus in the form of a swan. Helen of Troy was born from this union.

Megara: The wife of Heracles who he murdered in a fit of madness.

Melanthius: Goatherd servant of Odysseus who sides with the suitors and is mutilated for his treachery.

Melantho: Sister of Melanthius, mistress of Eurymachus. She is hanged along with the other females for her treachery and for her insults to Odysseus.

Menelaus: Son of Atreus, brother of Agamemnon and husband of Helen of Troy.

Mentes: King of the Taphians and very old friend of Odysseus.

Minos: King of Crete. Son of Zeus and Europa. Brother of Rhadymanthus and father of Sarpedon.

Myrmidons: The ferocious warriors who followed Achilles in the Trojan War.

Nausicaa: Phaeacian Princess. Daughter of Alcinous and Arete.

Neleus: Father of Nestor.

Neoptolemus: Son of Achilles and valiant warrior. He arrived to fight in Troy after his father's death and was presented with his father's armour by Odysseus.

Nestor: The aged yet still valiant king of Pylos. Famed for his sound advice, especially during the Trojan War.

Odysseus: King of Ithaca, husband of Penelope and father of Telemachus.

Orestes: Son of Agamemnon and Clytemnestra. He kills his mother and her lover after they murdered his father.

Orion: A mighty hunter, immortalised after his death by being placed in the sky as a constellation.

Otus: A youthful giant who with his twin Epialtes threatened battle with the gods.

Peleus: Father of Achilles.

Penelope: Wife of Odysseus and mother of Telemachus.

Pero: A great beauty. Daughter of Neleus king of Pylos and Chloris.

Phemius: The bard who is forced to sing by the suitors in the hall of Odysseus.

Philoetius: The cowherd on Ithaca who remains loyal to Odysseus.

Polycaste: Youngest daughter of Nestor.

Poseidon: God of the sea who prevents Odysseus returning to Ithaca after he kills the Cyclops.

Proteus: An ancient sea god who was known as the old man of the sea.

Rhadymanthus: Son of Zeus and Europa. After his death one of the judges of the dead in Hades.

Sheria: Fantastical isle of the Phaeacians.

Tiresias: The blind Theban seer who is called from Hades to give Odysseus advice on how to return home.

Telemachus: The son of Odysseus and Penelope.

Theoclymenus: A seer who predicts their impending doom to the suitors. He is ignored by them.

Illustrations

Cover illustration: Odysseus and his companions blinding Polyphemus. Original drawing by Tony Byrne, based on fifth century BC kraters.

p.7: Phemius, singing to the suitors (Odyssey, 1.153).

p.22: Nestor's sacrifice (Odyssey, 3.430).

p.125: The sirens (Odyssey, 12.184).

p.180: Odysseus and his dog (Odyssey, 17.292).

p.236: Odysseus killing the suitors (Odyssey, 22.122).

Apart from the cover all the illustrations are from John Flaxman, *The Odyssey of Homer*, engraved by T. Piroli from the compositions of John Flaxman, London, 1793. British Library G.769.(2). Reproduced by permission of the British Library Board.

CPSIA information can be obtained at www.ICGtesting.com
Printed in the USA
BVOW04*1128180813

328936BV00001B/19/P